Cameos
—Classical to Costume

Monica Lynn Clements
Patricia Rosser Clements

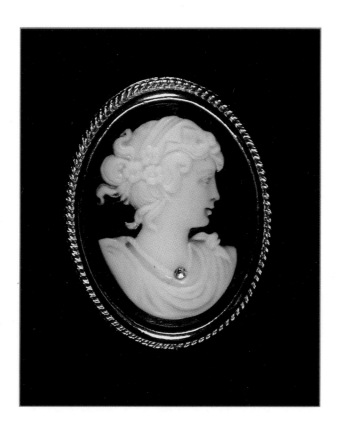

Schiffer Publishing Ltd

4880 Lower Valley Road, Atglen, PA 19310 USA

To our friend and personal cheerleader, Mary Moon.
Thanks for your motivation and words of wisdom—we dedicate this book to you.

Library of Congress Cataloging-in-Publication Data

Clements, Monica Lynn.
    Cameos: classical to costume/Monica Lynn Clements,
Patricia Rosser Clements.
        p. cm.
    Includes bibliographical references and index.
    ISBN 0-7643-0426-7 (hardcover)
    1. Cameos--Collectors and collecting. I. Clements,
Patricia Rosser. II. Title.
NK5720.C64 1998
736'.222-dc21   97-37937
                        CIP

Designed by "Sue"

ISBN: 0-7643-0426-7
Printed in China

Published by Schiffer Publishing Ltd.
4880 Lower Valley Road
Atglen, PA 19310
Phone: (610) 593-1777; Fax: (610) 593-2002
e-mail: schifferbk@aol.com
Please write for a free catalog.
This book may be purchased from the publisher.
Please include $3.95 for shipping.

Please try your bookstore first.

We are interested in hearing from authors
with book ideas on related subjects.

Acknowledgments

Our thanks to the people who allowed their cameos to be photographed for this book. We had the great pleasure of meeting collectors with entire collections or a single cameo that was a prized family heirloom. Thanks for opening your homes and shops to us.

Contents

Introduction

Cameos are a unique and always recognizable piece of jewelry. Their composition, subject, and history have provided collectors with many avenues of study. The cameo has endured from the days of stone, shell, and lava, and it continues to thrive in the present day.

In this book, we have presented a sampling of the endless variety of cameos that appeal to the collector. We have included a brief history to show the cameo's evolution from the Georgian period to the present day.

While we have attempted to group the cameos by material (i.e. stone, lava, shell, plastic, etc.) some cameos made of other materials may pop up in unexpected places. For example, a stone cameo may appear in the shell chapter. We have tried to keep this from happening as much as possible. Since many collectors we have met collect such an array of cameos, these pieces appear in the photographs. This variety makes the cameos more interesting to study.

The purpose of this book is not to set firm prices, but to be used as a guide. The prices of cameos reflect the combined experience of both authors in collecting and dealing in antique and collectible jewelry. The cameo prices are representative of the range of values observed throughout the United States and Europe.

Chapter One
The History of the Cameo

The study of the cameo is the study of history. Cameos provide clues to the past. In them, we can see the changing times through the subjects depicted and materials used, and we find some remarkable examples of craftsmanship.

The carving of cameos signified a change in the way people viewed jewelry. The cameo had no apparent purpose other than as an ornament. For example, cameos served as a setting in jewelry (a brooch or ring), a decoration on objects, or as sculpture.

The cameo first appeared around the time of Alexander the Great. This distinctive piece of jewelry has enjoyed popularity throughout Classical times, the Renaissance, and the eighteenth and nineteenth centuries. Even today, in the 1990s, there has been a resurgence of interest in the cameo.

Intaglios

Before the cameo, jewelry was functional. The intaglio, often used as a seal for documents or property, came before the cameo. The opposite of the cameo, the intaglio is a design carved below the surface. Common stones used for intaglios were beryl, onyx, and sardonyx.

Top: Onyx intaglio watch fob, ca. 1890. Gold frame is .75" in diameter. $395-425.
Bottom: Onyx intaglio slide on watch chain, ca. 1890. Gold frame, .75" x .75". $525-575.
The cameos in this photograph are *Courtesy of Shirley Falardeau.*

Cameos

Unlike the intaglio, the cameo stands out in relief. Early cameo carvers utilized such stones as agate, onyx, and sardonyx for their creations. Carvers cut away the top layer in relief and exposed the darker layer as the background. Through the changes and periods jewelry has undergone, carvers have looked to other materials for cameos such as coral, ivory, jet, lava, and shell.

Cameos can be molded from synthetic materials such as plastic or glass. Gutta-percha, Bakelite, and celluloid are examples of materials jewelry manufacturers have used for their cameo designs.

Top: Gold earrings with hardstone cameos of woman's portrait, ca. 1840. Frames with Etruscan style beading, .62" x .88". $300-400.
Center left: Hardstone cameo of woman set in bar pin, ca. 1880s. Frame has Etruscan style beading, 1.75" x .88". $500-600.
Bottom left: Stone cameo depicting an angel playing a lyre, locket/pendant, ca. 1920s. Gold with Etruscan style beading, 1.12" x 1.5". $900-1200.
Bottom right: 18" book chain/necklace with stone cameo of woman in profile, ca. 1840. 1" x 1.25". $1200-1500.
The cameos in this photograph are *Courtesy of Melissa A. Elrod.*

Amber pendent depicting mythological motif of Bacchante maiden, a follower of Dionysus (Bacchus), god of wine and fertility, with wreath of grapes and grape leaves in hair, ca. 1840. No frame, tortoiseshell bail, 1.62" x 2". *Courtesy of Melissa A. Elrod.* $1200-1500.

Amber glass cameo bracelet, ca. 1970s. Gold mesh bracelet with cameo measuring 1.25" x 1.88". $175-195.

Amber cameo pendant depicting mythological motif of Demeter (Ceres), goddess of the harvest, ca. 1915. Set in frame with gold links, 1.62" x 2", ca. 1915. *Courtesy of Melissa A. Elrod.* $425-500.

Amythest intaglio ring, ca. 1890. Gold metal ring measures .88" at top. *Courtesy of State Line Antiques Mall.* $95-175.

Amber glass intaglio pendant incised from back of piece, ca. late 1880s. Etruscan style beading on gold frame, 1.12" x 1.5", with overall measurement of piece 2.62". *Courtesy of Antiques By Daisy, Stock Exchange Antique Mall, Conroe, Texas.* $500-600.

High relief coral cameo brooch with tassels, ca. 1870s. Black enamel trim, Etruscan style beading, and intricate decorative work. Frame is 14K gold, 1.75" x 1.38", with tassels measuring 1.75". *Courtesy of Frank and Dorothy Everts*. $2500-3000.

Top: Coral cameo in carved relief depicting woman with flower, ca. 1890s. No frame, .62" x .75". $300-400.
Bottom: Coral cameo pendant with portrait of woman, ca. 1890s. Set in frame with beading, filigree chain, 1" x 1.3". $1500-2000.
The cameos in this photograph are *Courtesy of The Patrician Antiques*.

Coral brooch/necklace of woman in profile wearing beads, head ornament, and flowers in hair, ca. 1890s. Set in 14K gold frame, 1.5" x 1.75". *Courtesy of Jan White.* $2500-3000.

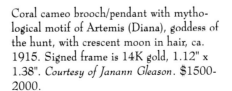

Coral cameo brooch/pendant with mythological motif of Artemis (Diana), goddess of the hunt, with crescent moon in hair, ca. 1915. Signed frame is 14K gold, 1.12" x 1.38". *Courtesy of Janann Gleason.* $1500-2000.

Top left: Coral ring of woman, ca. 1920s. Cameo measures .6" x .75". $800-950.

Top center: Coral ring with gold of woman in profile, ca. 1920s. Cameo measures .75" x 1.1". $2000-2500.

Top right: Coral cameo ring of woman in profile, ca. 1890s. Ornate setting, measures. 7" x .1". $925-1200.

Bottom left: Coral cameo ring of Classical figure, ca. 1920s. Measures .38" x .5". $750-795.

Bottom center: Coral cameo ring of Classical woman, ca. 1920s. Measures .75" x 1". $950-1200.

Bottom right: Coral cameo habillé ring of woman with flower in hair, ca. 1920s. Measures .38" x .88". $950-1200.

All cameo rings in this photograph are *Courtesy of The Patrician Antiques*.

Carved ivory pendant with scene, ca. 1890s. Set in frame of 24K gold, 1.75" x 2.5". *Courtesy of Melissa A. Elrod.* $2500-3000.

Gutta-percha cameo of woman's portrait with 30" chain, ca. 1890s. Measures 1.88" x 2.38". *Courtesy of Melissa A. Elrod.* $425-450.

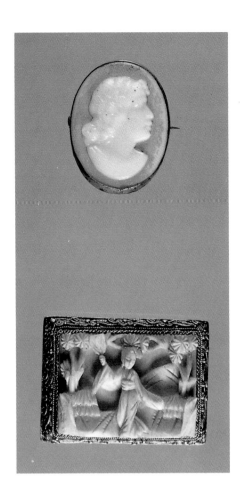

Top: Glass cameo, ca. 1850s. Gold metal frame, 1.12" x 1.38". $325-350.
Bottom: Rectangular ivory cameo brooch carved in deep relief, ca. 1900s. Gold frame, 1.75" x 1.3". $400-500.
The cameos in this photograph are *Courtesy of Kathleen Cunningham.*

Magnified view of carved ivory ring depicting woman's portrait, ca. 1880s. Set in gold frame. *Courtesy of Jackie McDonald.* $525-575.

Left: Ivory brooch of woman, ca. 1890. Backing is mother-of-pearl, 2" in diameter. $625-650.
Center: Ivory brooch/pendant with mythological motif of Artemis (Diana), goddess of the hunt, with crescent moon in her hair, ca. 1890s. No frame, 1.38" x 1.75". $725-795.
Right: Signed ivory brooch/pendant of woman in profile, ca. 1920s. Ornate gold frame with gold leaves, 1.88" x 2.25". $750-795.
The cameos in this photograph are *Courtesy of Melissa A. Elrod.*

Left: Jet cameo on carnelian background, ca. 1930s. Set in unusual frame, 1.88" x 2.62". $600-700.
Center: Jet portrait of a woman, ca. 1915. Set in heavy gold frame, 1.62" x 1.88". $800-900.
Right: Jet cameo on onyx, ca. 1890. Measures 2.25" x 3.12". $900-1200.
The cameos in this photograph are *Courtesy of Melissa A. Elrod*.

Jet cameo pendant depicting woman, ca. 1890s. No frame, 2.38" x 2.88". *Courtesy of The Patrician Antiques*. $395-425.

Jet cameo brooch has portrait of woman, ca. 1890s. No frame, embossed work at corners of brooch, 1.62" x 2". $425-450.

Shell cameo brooch mythological motif of Demeter (Ceres), goddess of the harvest, with stalks of grain, ca. 1860. Gold frame with twisted wire and beads and c clasp, 2.38" x 3". *Courtesy of Melissa A. Elrod.* $600-750.

Lava carving in high relief depicting mythological motif of the head of Artemis (Diana), goddess of the hunt, ca. 1810. Mounted on velvet in modern frame, cameo measures 1" x 1.25". *Courtesy of Frank and Dorothy Everts.* $625-650.

Jet necklace with opal cameo on jet background, ca. 1880. 14K gold beads, cameo has 14K gold frame, 1.5" x 2". *Courtesy of Antiques By Daisy.* $3000-4000.

18th Century

Cameo Portraits in Wax

The practice of modeling wax portraits goes back to the fourth century B.C. This method of working with wax became popular with sculptors and artists as a way to perfect their work before the actual carving of stone or painting on canvas began. Cameo carvers employed wax in a similar way and produced model portraits before they began to fashion their designs in their chosen material.

For people who could not afford to buy a cameo, a wax portrait was the next best thing to collect and to study. At different times throughout the seventeenth and eighteenth century, these portraits enjoyed popularity. The art of wax portraiture died out in the nineteenth century.[1]

Wax cameo portrait in high relief depicting Classical woman's portrait, ca. 1750. Mounted in modern frame, measures 1.38" x 1.62". *Courtesy of Frank and Dorothy Everts*. Museum quality.

Making plaster impressions of carved and engraved gems reached its peak in the eighteenth century. These durable plaster of paris impressions made up the important collections of churches and governments who studied the significance of the designs. Another purpose of the impressions was to provide a record of carved and engraved gems.[2]

These casts offer an important link to the past. Examining them gives insight into the style and the variety of subjects past engravers and carvers chose. The designs show what appealed to the collectors of long ago. While such casts are rare, they can be found in museums or in private collections.

The following pages illustrate plaster cast impressions of carved and engraved gems. These casts show the designs of religious and mythological motifs as well as portraiture, ca. 1750. *Courtesy of Frank and Dorothy Everts.* Museum quality.

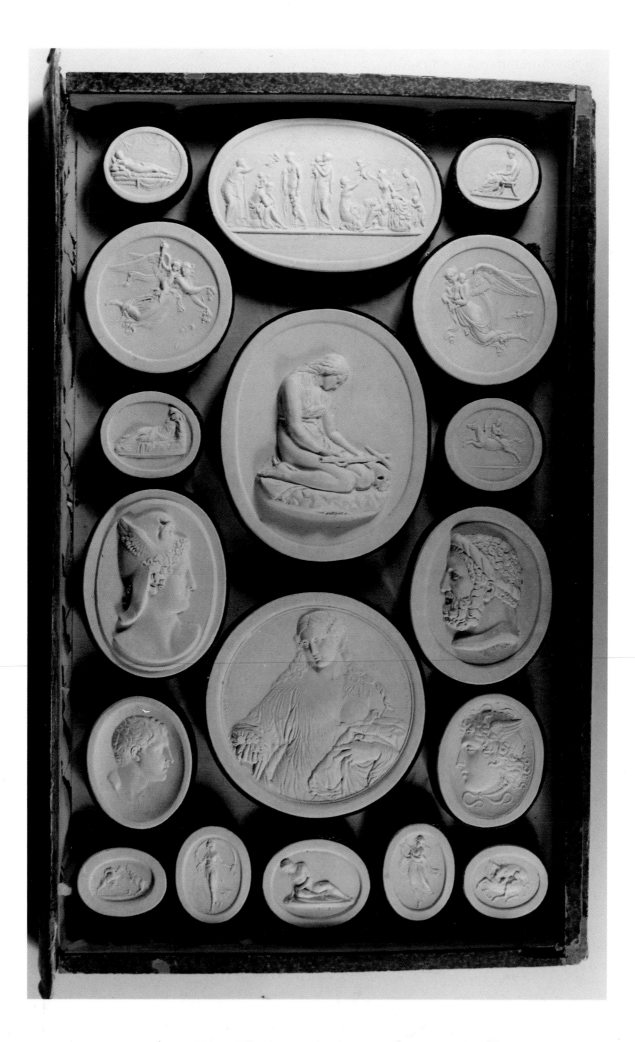

20

23

Artisans of the eighteenth century joined cameos together by gold chains forming panels. Bracelets with cameo clasps became fashionable, but the ring was considered most fashionable. Cameo rings from this period became popular.

Schools of engraving appeared as the result of an insatiable passion for engraved gems that swept Europe in the eighteenth century. With the rush to make cameos, many carvers did not exert the same care in craftsmanship. Less scrupulous carvers took the opportunity to create fraudulent pieces and forged signatures of well known carvers on the backs of cameos. Novice collectors could not differentiate between the real and the fake. Producing copies of older cameos became the livelihood of some carvers.

Glass

Glass cameos reached their zenith in the late eighteenth century. James Tassie (1735-1799), a Scotsman, developed a glass paste that he used with great success to imitate gems carved into intaglios and cameos. It was difficult to identify the real jewelry from the faux creations.

Tassie's castings were copies of ancient cameos and intaglios. The subjects ranged from a variety of mythological motifs to portraits of royals or wealthy figures of the day. His reproductions did not have a plaster look and mirrored "the transparency or opacity as well as the color and workmanship of the originals."[3] With his ability to gain access to the great collections of Europe, his casts numbered 15,800.[4]

After Tassie's death, his nephew, William, took over the business of producing cameos from glass paste. This business continued into the 1800s, until William's death, when the production of Tassie cameos diminished. Through his work in offering an affordable cameo, Tassie changed jewelry forever as the masses could indulge in a pastime that was once reserved for the wealthy.

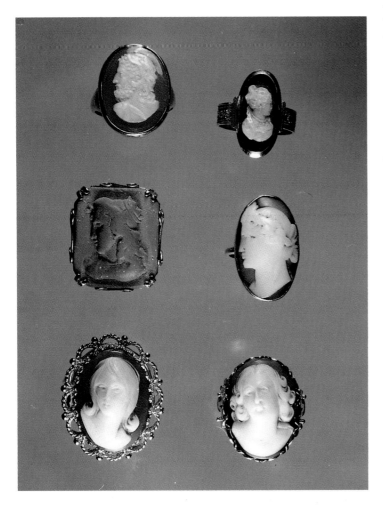

Top left: Sardonyx cameo ring of bearded man, ca. late 1700s. Set in gold frame, .75" x 1". $2000-3000.
Top right: Sardonyx cameo ring of woman in profile, ca. early 1800s. Set in gold frame, .55" x .88". $1500-2000.
Center left: Lava ring of Roman woman in profile, ca. early 1800s. Set in gold frame, 1" x 1.12". $800-1200.
Center right: Sardonyx shell cameo (with a greenish cast) of an emperor, possibly Tiberius, wearing a wreath, ca. late 1700s. Set in gold frame, .75" x 1.12". $3000-4000.
Bottom left: Shell cameo of anonymous woman, ca. 1900s. Set in beaded and decorated gold frame, 1.12" x 1.3". $400-600.
Bottom right: Shell cameo ring, ca. 1900s. Set in gold frame, .88" x 1.12" . $600-700.
The cameos in this photograph are *Courtesy of Melissa A. Elrod.*

Like Tassie, Josiah Wedgwood (1730-1795) sold attractive, affordable cameos. In England, he produced beautiful ceramic cameos and sent many of his pieces to France for setting. These cameos retained a romantic charm that other cameos of the period lacked.

After developing the process for making the jaspar ware cameo, Wedgwood decided that this material was what he preferred for his cameos. To create the jasper ware cameo, a white stoneware cameo was fashioned onto on a light blue ceramic background and then joined into one piece through a firing process. The blue color of his pieces has become known as Wedgwood blue. Wedgwood cameos come in a variety of colors, and their manufacture continues to the present.

Top left: Signed Wedgwood jasper ware cameo pendant, ca. early 1900s. Sterling silver frame and bail, .63" x 1". $425-450.
Top right: Signed Wedgwood jasper ware cameo brooch/pendant depicting mythological motif of Eros (Cupid), ca. early 1900s. Gold frame, 1.25" in diameter. $395-425.
Bottom: Signed Wedgwood jasper ware cameo brooch/pendant, ca. early 1900s. Sterling silver with 10K gold wreath frame, 1.50" in diameter. $425-450.

Opposite page:
Left: Blue Tassie cameo (pate-de-verre) of woman, ca. 1860s. Twisted gold wire frame with Etruscan style beading,1.75" x 2.12". $525-550.
Center: Wedgwood jasper ware cameo earrings depicting mythological motif of the muse, Melpomene, the singer, with the mask and club of Hercules, ca. early 1900s. Gold frame, .5" x .88". $225-250.
Right: Wedgwood jasper ware cameo brooch depicting mythological motif of the muse, Melpomene, the singer, with the mask of Hercules, ca. early 1890s. Gold beaded frame, 1.38" x 1.12". $825-850.
The cameos in this photograph are *Courtesy of Melissa A. Elrod.*

Signed Wedgwood pendant, ca. early 1900s. Gold frame, .62" in diameter. *Courtesy of Lenora Alice Knighton.* $350-425.

19th Century

France

When Napoleon Bonaparte came to power in France in 1804, the members of his court enjoyed displaying and wearing engraved gems. Napoleon and the French loved cameos and did not care whether the pieces were old or new. The French emperor showed his admiration for the cameo when he commissioned furniture and other objects to be made and adorned with cameos. While this custom no doubt contributed to the opulent atmosphere, it gave the cameo a mass produced look.

Empress Josephine, Napoleon's wife, wore a crown studded with cameos at Napoleon's coronation. Josephine loved to wear engraved gems. Many women of the French court adorned themselves with similar cameo jewelry. Napoleon gave Empress Josephine a parure set described as having "eighty-two antique cameos surrounded by 275 pearls."[5]

Examples of the kind of jewelry Josephine made popular were cameos "linked by chains of gold or pearls to make necklaces, earrings, bracelets and set in tiaras and decorative combs."[6]

Shell

During the early nineteenth century, French and Italian carvers used shell to create cameos. Carvers discovered Black Helmet and Queen's Conch shells in abundance for their work. Shell was soft and could be carved quickly, so it became a favorite material for producing cameos to meet the high demand. Empress Josephine especially treasured cameos made of shell, and her favor made this type of cameo popular in France.

Left: Rebecca at the Well cameo brooch/pendant, ca. 1880s. Set in etched gold frame, 1.75" x 2.12". $900-1200.
Top center: High relief portrait of woman, ca. early 1800s. Set in heavy gold frame with twisted wire and c clasp, measures 1.12" x 1.3". $700-900.
Lower center: Cameo brooch portrait in relief of woman with flowers in her hair, ca. 1860s. Set in frame with Etruscan style beading, measures 1.5" x 1.88". $900-1200.
Right: Cameo pendant with portrait of woman wearing necklace, ca. 1890s. Set in frame with Etruscan style beading, measures 1.62" x 2". $800-900.
The cameos in this photograph are *Courtesy of Bobby and Mary Fyffe.*

The Influence of Archaeological Discoveries

Excavations of ancient sites in the early nineteenth century renewed an interest in jewelry of the past. Findings at Pompeii in 1806 and an interest in such sites as Herculaneum fueled the enthusiasm. Discoveries in Etruscan tombs helped create a revival of ancient jewelry.

A characteristic of this jewelry that appears on the frames of many cameos is the Etruscan style granulation or beading. Carvers looked to the archaeological jewelry for the subjects of their work. Cameo motifs of this period show the influence of Classical designs through the carved images of gods and goddesses from Classical mythology.

The interest in ancient history and the growth of tourism in Europe boosted the demand for cameos. As tourists traveled to Italy during the eighteenth century and nineteenth century, they found a wide selection of cameos from which to choose. The compact size of the cameo made it an ideal souvenir, and tourists could readily purchase carvings of shell, stone, or lava. Mythological motifs continued to be popular subjects, and personal portraits commissioned by travelers became the vogue.

Lava

Mt. Vesuvius was the source of lava that allowed carvers to produce an inexpensive and distinctive looking cameo for souvenir hunters during the nineteenth century. The lava cameos came in such colors as white, black, cream, and olive green. The softness of the lava gave artists a perfect medium to design intricate carvings in high relief.

Left: Rectangular shell cameo brooch of Grecian woman, ca. 1790s. Twisted gold frame measures 1.75" x 2". $1200-1500.
Right: Shell cameo pendant with mythological motif of Bacchante maiden, follower of Dionysus (Bacchus), god of wine and fertility, with wreath of grapes and leaves in her hair, ca. 1840-60. Frame is 14K gold, 1.75" x 2.25". $1500-2500.
The cameos in this photograph are *Courtesy of Melissa A. Elrod.*

Top left: Loose lava cameo in relief depicting mythological motif of Hermes (Mercury), messenger for the gods, portrayed with wings on hat, ca. 1860. Mounted on velvet in wooden tray. $425-475.
Top center: Loose lava cameo portrait in high relief of Classical woman, ca. 1830. Mounted on velvet in wooden tray. $350-395.
Right: Loose lava cameo in high relief depicting mythological motif of the woodland god, Pan, with reed pipe, ca. 1840. Mounted on velvet in wooden tray. $425-450.
Bottom left: Loose lava cameo portrait of angel in high relief, ca. 1830. Mounted on velvet in wooden tray. $475-495.

Bottom center: Loose lava cameo portrait in high relief depicting mythological motif of Bacchante maiden, a follower of Dionysus (Bacchus), god of wine and fertility, ca. 1830. mounted on velvet in wooden tray. $475-495.
Bottom right: Loose lava cameo in relief depicting mythological motif of Artemis (Diana), goddess of the hunt, with crescent moon on her head, ca. 1830. Mounted on velvet in wooden tray. $425-450.
The cameos in the photograph are *Courtesy of Frank and Dorothy Everts.*

While the lava cameo was an inexpensive souvenir for visitors to Italy, these detailed pieces of jewelry were a status symbol for women of the day. A lava cameo signified that a woman had traveled to Italy on the Grand Tour. Today, these carvings in lava continue to be collectible. Dating a cameo can be a challenge, but with a lava cameo, one can say with a great deal of certainty that it originated in the nineteenth century.

Black lava cameo high relief carving depicting mythological motif of Eros (Cupid) with bow and arrows, ca. 1830. Mounted on velvet background, cameo measures 1.12" x 1.38". *Courtesy of Frank and Dorothy Everts.* $375-450.

Lava cameo in high relief depicting mythological motif of Demeter (Ceres), goddess of the harvest, holding stalks of wheat, ca. 1830. Mounted on velvet in modern frame, some damage to bottom center and bottom right of carving, 1.5" x 1.88". *Courtesy of Frank and Dorothy Everts.* $325-350.

Profile of Eros (Cupid) to show detail of high relief carving, ca. 1830. Mounted on velvet background. *Courtesy of Frank and Dorothy Everts.* $375-475.

England

When Queen Victoria ascended the British throne in 1837, the Victorian Era, as we now call it, began. The queen enjoyed wearing jewelry and liked to give pieces of jewelry as gifts. Shell cameo brooches and earrings were favorites of Queen Victoria throughout her reign and thereby ensured their lasting popularity.

Women were not the only ones who enjoyed wearing cameos. Men wore rings set with cameos or intaglios. Pins with scarves and watch fobs that included cameos or intaglios were common accessories of the day.

Onyx cameo ring with two profiles, ca. 1867. Frame is 14K gold, pictured life size. *Courtesy of Pat Abernathy.* $350-450.

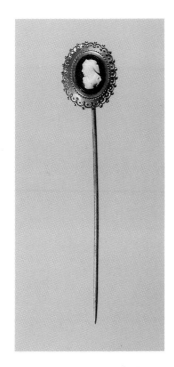

Stickpin with stone cameo, ca. 1850. Frame decorated with Etruscan style beading. $195-225.

Top left: Stone cameo locket, ca. 1890s. Cameo set in etched frame against octagonal pinchbeck frame, 1.25" x 1.75". $400-600.
Top right: Loose Cupid made of lava, ca. 1870s. Carved in relief, slight damage to top left of carving, .88" x 1.12". $200-300.
Bottom: Glass cameo depicting woman, ca. early 1900s. Set in gold frame, 2" x 2.45". $300-400.
The cameos in this photograph are *Courtesy of The Patrician Antiques.*

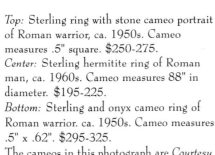

Top: Sterling ring with stone cameo portrait of Roman warrior, ca. 1950s. Cameo measures .5" square. $250-275.
Center: Sterling hermitite ring of Roman man, ca. 1960s. Cameo measures 88" in diameter. $195-225.
Bottom: Sterling and onyx cameo ring of Roman warrior. ca. 1950s. Cameo measures .5" x .62". $295-325.
The cameos in this photograph are *Courtesy of Judith E. Williams.*

Left: Onyx cameo ring with Roman warrior wearing helmet, ca. 1860. Ring 14K gold, cameo measures .62" x .75". *Courtesy of J. Marie Reed.* $595-625.
Right: Stone cameo pendant, ca. 1990s. Silver frame, .88" x 1". *Courtesy of Valery Owen.* $225-295.

Popular Motifs

Along with cameos depicting mythological figures, other designs embellished the cameo. Flowers were a popular subject for cameos of the 1800s. Victorians had a keen interest in horticulture. The many books and magazines of the period are indicative of this fact. The result of this interest appears in Victorian jewelry. Cameo designs depicted the floral motif through a variation on the bouquet or a hand holding a bouquet of flowers. Flowers continued to be a common subject for cameo brooches until the present day.

The subject of Rebecca at the Well grew into popularity in the 1860s. This design, taken from the Biblical reference, portrayed a scene including a well, a house, and a woman. The design of the cameo varied according to the carver. Some cameo artists created a detailed carving with trees or bushes in the background while other carvers preferred to create a light, dreamy scene with little depth to the carving. Cameo carvers depicted this motif on brooches, pendants, rings, and earrings.

Top: Rebecca at the Well shell cameo pendant, ca. 1890s. Set in beautiful filigree frame with four roses, 1.7" x 2.12". $700-800.
Bottom left: Rebecca at the Well cameo, ca. 1890s. No frame, 1.38" x 1.7". $375-395.
Bottom right: Rebecca at the Well pendant/locket, ca. 1890s. Gold frame, 1.38" x 1.62". $800-1200.
The cameos in this photograph are *Courtesy of The Patrician Antiques.*

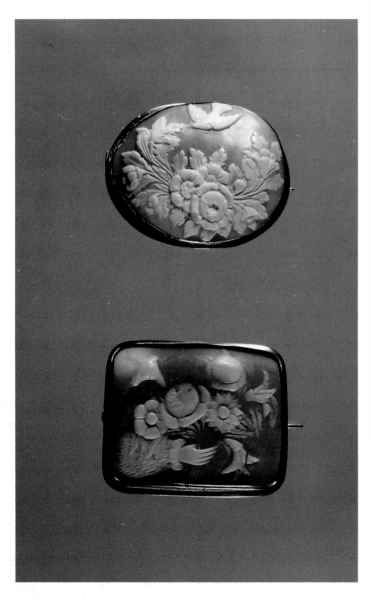

Top: Oval shell cameo brooch depicting floral motif with bird, ca. 1850s. Set in gold frame, 2" x 1.5". $800-1000.
Bottom: Rectangular shell cameo brooch depicting floral motif of hand holding bouquet, ca. 1890s. Set in gold frame, 2" x 1.62". $800-1000.
Courtesy of Frank and Dorothy Everts.

Coral

The discovery of an abundance of coral near the seaside town of Torre del Greco, Italy, heralded the production of coral jewelry during the nineteenth century. Victorians believed in the power of coral and thought it could ward off evil. Coral jewelry was plentiful and flourished well into the 1860s. Children wore coral beads, and parures of coral were popular with Victorian ladies.

Made of the skeletons of marine animals, coral is a calcium carbonate substance in a wide range of colors in pinks and reds as well as white and black. Like shell and lava, carvers found coral to possess a quality of softness that made it easy to work with. Carvers created a variety of designs. The dark reds and pinks of coral were the colors sought after by collectors.

Magnified view of coral cameo pendant carved in high relief depicting woman adorned with flowers and wearing necklace, ca. 1850s. Frame is gold, 1.12" x 1.25". *Courtesy of Bobby and Mary Fyffe*. $1500-2000.

Side view of the coral cameo pendant to illustrate the high relief and quality of the carving. *Courtesy of Bobby and Mary Fyffe*.

Mass Production

With the mass production of jewelry during the late nineteenth century, the demand for jewelry became strong. The cameo was more popular than ever. The effect of such demand resulted in the cameo portrait of generalized women. These cameo designs of women became common subjects that surpassed the mythological motifs.

Left: Shell cameo brooch, ca. 1890. Gold frame with Etruscan style beading, 1.75" x 2.25". $600-800.
Right: Shell cameo pendant of woman with flower in her hair, ca. 1880s. Set in beaded and engraved gold frame, 1.38" x 1.62". $400-500.
The cameos in this photograph are *Courtesy of Jackie McDonald*.

The portrait of generalized women caused an augmentation in the features of women depicted in cameos. The silhouette of a Roman woman with a long, straight nose was typical of the early nineteenth century. Around 1850, women traveling to Italy desired a cameo with more modern features. Carvers began producing designs of women's portraits with an upturned nose, more elaborate hairstyles, and portraits that included women wearing jewelry.

Detractors have equated the appearance of the unknown women with a decline in craftsmanship and a loss of imagination by the cameo carvers. This criticism has not affected the popularity of this design. The unknown women have changed over the years, yet they have endured.

Cameo Habillé

Artisans of the nineteenth century created a slightly different look to the unknown woman's portrait with the cameo habillé. The woman herself was shown wearing a necklace and/or other jewelry such as earrings or a diadem of small diamonds. Throughout the years, the jewelry on this type of cameo has taken on different styles with a variation of the diamonds and their arrangement in the portrait. Like the portrait of the unknown woman, the cameo habillé is a design produced in the present day.

The work of cameo copiers in a broad range of new materials had an adverse effect on jewelry in the nineteenth century. The upper classes felt horrified that affordable fakes and copies allowed the masses to wear expensive looking jewelry. The stone and shell cameo industry diminished because their prices were too high for the growing market. Jewelry collectors who realized how they had been fooled by fakes and forgeries lost interest in collecting cameo jewelry.

Left: Shell cameo habillé with diamond of woman with flowers in hair and on shoulder, ca. 1880s. Silver filigree frame, 1.75" x 2.12". $600-800.
Right: Shell cameo habillé with diamond depicting woman with flowers in hair and butterfly on shoulder, ca. 1890s. Silver frame, 1.62" x 2.12". $500-700.
The cameos in this photograph are *Courtesy of Angelia Jones*.

20th Century

The original quality of master stone and shell carvers gave way to cameos that required little thought to design. The production of shell and stone cameos continued to a lesser degree after World War II. Inexpensive jewelry became popular with the use of synthetic materials and inexpensive metals. Celluloids, Bakelite, gutta-percha, jet, and amber were among the materials used in making cameos during the early years of the 20th century.

Milkglass cameo brooch/pendant, ca. 1860-80. Gold frame with Etruscan style beading, 2.5" x 2". *Courtesy of Antiques By Daisy.* $225-325.

Top: Shell cameo brooch, ca. 1940s. Twisted gold frame, 1" x 1.25". $300-400.

Center: Shell cameo earrings, ca. 1950s. Twisted ribbon effect on frame, .66" x .88". $250-350.

Bottom: Shell cameo intricately carved with profile of pretty woman with flowers on shoulder and in hair, ca. early 1900s. Gold frame has Etruscan style beading, 1.5" x 2". $600-800.

The cameos in this photograph are *Courtesy of Mary Sax.*

Celluloid cameo pendant necklace of woman with flower in hair and on shoulder, ca. 1890s. Measures 2.12" x 2.75". *Courtesy of The Patrician Antiques.* $225-295.

Left: Celluloid cameo brooch with portrait of woman, ca. 1890. Frame with c clasp, 2.12" x 2.75". $125-175.

Right: Glass clip cameo in beaded and filigree frame with a motif from mythology depicting Aphrodite (Venus) with her mother, Dione, ca. 1915. Silver frame, 1.88" x 2.5". $165-195.

The cameos in this photograph are *Courtesy of Melissa A. Elrod.*

While the unknown woman continued to be a popular design for cameo artists, cameo portraits of the twentieth century took on a different look from the older pieces. Carvers modernized the features of the anonymous women. The noses in the designs now depicted a more upturned and sometimes pert look. The hairstyles changed with the times from long and flowing romantic look to a shorter style with waves or curls.

Late 20th Century

Cameo production changed in the mid-twentieth century. Shortages of materials and resources to produce jewelry drastically affected the making of shell cameos. Their production came to a virtual standstill in Italy while in the United States, renewed patriotism created an atmosphere of thrift that influenced fashion. Costume jewelry became the vogue, and manufacturers began to produce lovely costume jewelry, including cameo designs.

Jewelry manufacturers met the demand and offered attractive, affordable cameos. Plastic and clear glass jewelry of molded designs were plentiful. While these cameos did not have the same craftsmanship of the carved shell and stone cameos, they had their own style and enjoyed popularity.

Green glass cameo brooch with faux emeralds, ca. 1980s. Gold twisted wire on glass and back, 2" x 2.5". *Courtesy of Antiques By Daisy.* $175-195.

Signed Art blue glass with pearls and rhinestones of woman with flowing hair, ca. 1960s. Earrings are 1.2" in diameter, and brooch is 2.5" x 2.5". *Courtesy of Melissa A. Elrod.* $450-495.

Plastic white on coral colored cameo brooch, ca. 1960s. Gold frame, 1.5" x 2" *Courtesy of Mansion on Main Bed and Breakfast.* $55-75.

Camexco Made in Italy mother-of-pearl cameo set with box, ca. 1960s. Ring at top measures .75" x .88", earrings set in silver are .7" x .88", and brooch/pendant is .88" x 1". *Courtesy of Evelyn Kacos.* $275-325.

Left: Glass intaglio brooch incised from back, ca. 1970s. Set in gold metal frame, 1.75" x 2.25". $55-75.
Right: Heart shaped brooch with glass intaglio, ca. 1960s. Gold metal frame has seed pearls, 1.5" x 1.5". $125-150.
The cameos in this photograph are *Courtesy of Lorene Goetsch, Way Out West Mall, West, Texas.*

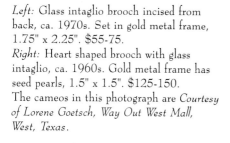

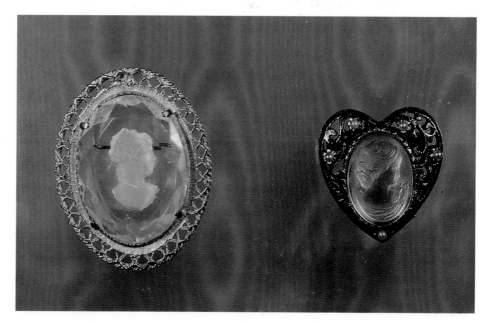

Left: Plastic white on blue cameo brooch/pendant with woman looking in mirror, ca. 1980s. Gold metal frame 1.5" x 2". $45-65.
Center: Plastic brooch/pendant with portrait of woman, ca. 1980s. Gold frame with pearls, 1.62" x 2". $55-75.
Right: Plastic white on pink woman looking in mirror, ca. 1980s. Gold metal frame with twisted effect, 1.5" x 1.75". *Courtesy of Sarah Newton.* $45-65.

Cameo Production Today

With a renewed interest in shell cameos, carvers work in the 1990s to create beautiful pieces with exquisite detail. The center of shell cameo production is the picturesque coastal town of Torre Del Greco, Italy. Here, carvers create shell cameos in a variety of different designs.

The proximity of Torre del Greco, located on the coast of Italy and at the foot of Mt. Vesuvius, caused the town to benefit from an abundance of lava, coral, and shell. It was inevitable that this seaside town would become the world center of cameo design. A carving school began in 1878, and the artisans of Torre del Greco embraced the art of producing cameos.

One example of a company that continues the art of cameo design is the Di Luca Brothers. This firm employs eighty-five carvers who follow the esteemed tradition which began with the early carvers. The beautiful designs of the shell cameos cover a wide variety of subjects from portraits of women to mythological scenes.

Whiting Davis set, ca. 1960s. Cameo clip-on earrings .88" in diameter, cameo pendant 1.88" in diameter with 22" chain. Cameos set in silver metal mesh frames. *Courtesy of Lorene Goetsch.* $175-195.

Opposite page:
Shell cameos representing the variety of portraits and scenes produced by the talented carvers at the firm of Di Luca Brothers. *Courtesy of Di Luca Brothers.*

The work of the carvers at this company shows the modernization of cameos in the 1990s. An interesting aspect of the carvings is the change in the motif of the generalized woman. The designs now show women in motion or with long, flowing hair that blows in the breeze. When choosing subjects for their work, the carvers at Di Luca select designs that will appeal to their customers around the world.

Created by Benito Ruontolo, this cameo carving utilizes two contrasting colors of the shell. This design is popular in the Japanese cameo market. *Courtesy of Di Luca Brothers.*

Round shell cameo entitled "Adam and Eve," carved by Francesco Scala, a talented cameo artist at the Di Luca Brothers. *Courtesy of Di Luca Brothers.*

This shell cameo, carved by Alfonso Imperatrice, utilizes the soft contrasts in color to create the design of a woman with flowers. *Courtesy of Di Luca Brothers.*

A company once located in Torre del Greco, Tagliamonte now makes its home in Vicenza, Northern Italy. Tagliamonte brings a Classical yet modern look to their designs with colorful cameo and intaglio jewelry made of glass pastes. The lavastoneware cameos are reminiscent of the look and the designs of the Victorian era.

Courtesy of Nino Tagliamonte.

Tagliamonte has returned to the process began by early Romans as well as James Tassie in creating cameos and intaglios. The subjects for these cameos are Classical, yet this jewelry has a certain sophistication that makes it sought after by clients all over the world.

Courtesy of Nino Tagliamonte.

Courtesy of Nino Tagliamonte.

Courtesy of Nino Tagliamonte.

Opposite page:

The lavastone cameos are colorful and distinctive, yet they capture the beauty of lava cameos of the eighteenth and nineteenth centuries. The designers at Tagliamonte have discovered a method of creating a material that is the equivalent of lava. These cameo artists use the process created for the jasper ware cameo by Josiah Wedgwood. The designs of the cameos are Classical in style, and the colors and high relief make them unique and collectible.

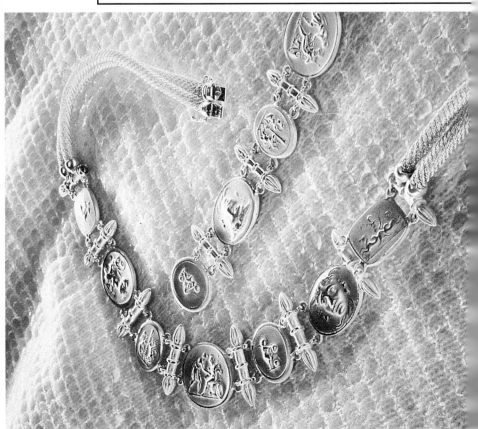

Courtesy of Nino Tagliamonte.

41

Courtesy of Nino Tagliamonte.

Courtesy of Nino Tagliamonte.

Courtesy of Nino Tagliamonte.

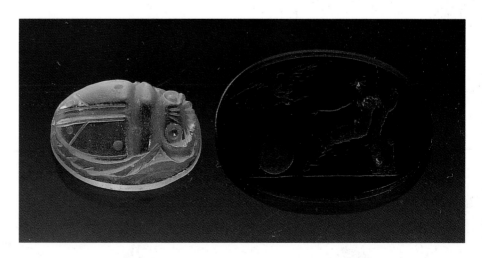

Courtesy of Nino Tagliamonte.

43

Studying Cameos

Studying cameos is especially rewarding for an individual with a keen interest in history and art. As one handles cameos, it becomes possible to identify the period and material of each cameo or intaglio. Discovering a cameo's material, how it looks, and how it feels is an important part of its history. The quality of the carving and its appeal will help determine whether it should become part of a collection.

Examining a cameo through magnification is vital for discerning the composition of the cameo and its setting or frame. The metal or other material used in the setting and the design are clues in dating a cameo. The metal alloy, pinchbeck, is a substance to look for, and search for the marks that identify gold or silver content. Sometimes, the metal work is exquisite and signed by the carver or manufacturer. Signatures on the backs of cameos may require some extra research, and the need to consult an expert may be indicated to identify one of the many forged signatures of expert cameo carvers.

Judging the cameo or intaglio by its quality, whether the piece is antique or contemporary, is important. Look at the carving carefully and handle many cameos to learn to identify a shell or stone cameo.

Cameos are interesting accents to clothing, and the plastic and glass cameos are fun to wear because they are durable and inexpensive. Found in antique shops and at estate sales, many old cameos are set in beautiful Victorian or Art Nouveau frames. More recent cameos are quite collectible and readily available.

Notes

[1] Miller, p. 136-137.
[2] Miller, p. 138.
[3] Henig, Martin, p. 384.
[4] Henig, Martin, p. 384.
[5] Gere, Charlotte, p. 206.
[6] Gere, Charlotte, p. 28.

Top left: Shell cameo earrings with portrait of woman, ca. 1990s. Set in silver frames, measure .88" in diameter. $300-400.
Bottom left: Old style glass cameo earrings with portraits of woman ca. 1990s. Ornate frames measure 1.25" x 1.88. $75-95.
Right: Shell cameo earrings with portrait of woman, ca. 1990s. Ornate frames with garnet stones and old style filigree measure 1.25" x 2.25". $325-500.
The cameos in this photograph are *Courtesy of Melissa A. Elrod.*

Avon white on black plastic cameo habillé pendant with stone, ca.
1980. Gold tone frame has twisted effect, 1.38" x 1.75". *Courtesy of
Lenora Alice Knighton*. $65-85.

Chapter Two
Stone

Top: Onyx cameo earrings, ca. 1890. Sterling silver frame. $200-300.

Bottom: Onyx cameo clasp on jet necklace, ca. 1890. Sterling silver frame on clasp, 1.25" x 1.5". $500-600.

The cameos in this photograph are *Courtesy of Great Finds & Designs, Inc. of Texarkana.*

Onyx cameo brooch/pendant intricately carved, ca. early 1800s. Frame 18K gold with Etruscan style granulation, 1.5" x 1.75". *Courtesy of Buhrman-Pharr Gifts.* $2500-3500.

Top: Onyx cameo brooch of woman, ca. early 1800s. Gold frame, 1" x 1.12" $500-595.

Center left: Onyx cameo portrait depicting mythological portrait of Hermes (Mercury), messenger for the gods, ca. 1890s. Measures 1" in diameter. $1200-1500.

Center right: Classical portrait of woman in profile, ca. 1860. Carved in agate with onyx background, 1.12" x 1.5". $700-800.

Bottom: Onyx inlaid portrait of woman in silhouette, ca. 1920s. Set in gold Etruscan style beaded frame, 1.5" x 1.88". $325-500.

The cameos in this photograph are *Courtesy of Melissa A. Elrod*.

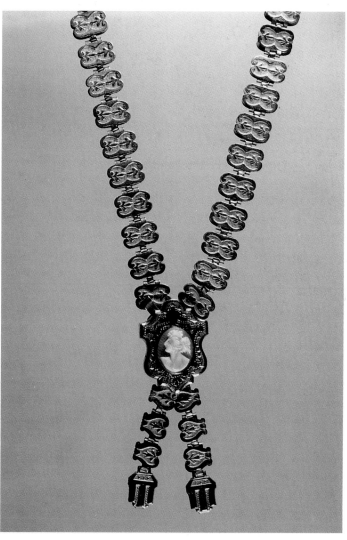

Book chain with stone cameo portrait, ca. 1850. Gold chain measures 10.5" and cameo is .75" x 1.25". *Courtesy of Jackie McDonald*. $800-1200.

Back of onyx cameo brooch/pendant, ca. early 1800s. Frame 18K gold, Etruscan style granulation, 1.5" x 1.75". *Courtesy of Buhrman-Pharr Gifts*. $2500-3500.

Onyx intaglio earrings, ca. 1930s. Gold metal modified clip-on backs, .75" x 1". *Courtesy of Garden Gate Antiques.* $225-295.

Rectangular brooch with cameos of two faces depicting night and day in black and white onyx, ca. 1840. Gold frame, .88" x 1". *Courtesy of Nana Dodds.* $500-600.

Stone cameo pendant of woman in profile marked Lidz Bros. NYC, ca. 1950s. Ornate frame with mother-of-pearl stones along with beading and filigree. Two stones missing on the right. 1.75" x 2.25". *Courtesy of Margaret McRaney.* $225-295 as is.

Stone cameo necklace, ca. 1840. Gold frame has seed pearls and twisted wire, 1" x 1.25". *Courtesy of Shirley Falardeau.* $500-600.

Stone cameo necklace in high relief, ca.
1890. 14K gold frame has twisted wire,
1.12" x 1.62". *Courtesy of Carol Allen
Poulos*. $1500-1800.

Onyx cameo pendant/locket depicting Classical figure, ca. 1840-60.
Gold metal with seed pearls and Etruscan style granulation on frame
with locket smaller than frame, 1.5" x 1.62" overall. *Courtesy of
Sarah Newton*. $400-600.

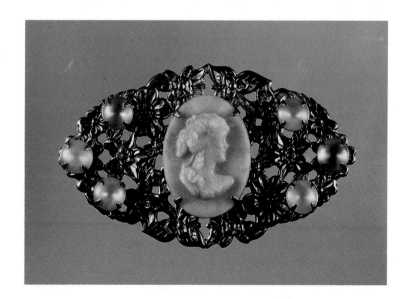

Distinctive brooch with stone cameo, ca. 1920s. Frame decorated
with interwoven flowers and leaves, glass stones set in frame, 3.25" x
1.88". *Courtesy of The Patrician Antiques*. $900-1200.

Heritage obsidian cameo watch/pendant, ca. late 1900s. Gold tone watch and frame with pearls around cameo, 1.38" in diameter, tassel measures 1". *Courtesy of Kenneth L. Surratt, Jr.* $125-175.

Top: Cameo stone ring with portrait of woman, ca. 1890. Set in ornate gold frame, .75" x 1.25". $325-425.
Bottom: Cameo brooch of stone depicting woman in profile, ca. 1900-1910. Set in gold frame decorated with leaves, 1.25" x 1.75". $300-400.
The cameos in this photograph are *Courtesy of Charlee Buford.*

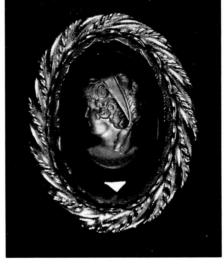

Onyx intaglio clip, ca. 1930. Silver frame with wreath design, 1" x 1.25". *Courtesy of Judith M. Davis.* $95-150.

Stone cameo brooch/pendant depicting mythological motif of Demeter (Ceres) goddess of the harvest, ca. 1890s. Octagonal frame is 14K gold with Etruscan style beading, 1" x 1.25". *Courtesy of Camille Crank McGinnis.* $900-1200.

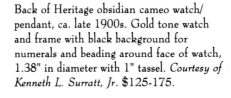

Back of Heritage obsidian cameo watch/pendant, ca. late 1900s. Gold tone watch and frame with black background for numerals and beading around face of watch, 1.38" in diameter with 1" tassel. *Courtesy of Kenneth L. Surratt, Jr.* $125-175.

Molded plastic cameo pendant on onyx, ca. 1950. Gold tone frame, 1.62" x 2". $55-75.

Signed Whiting Davis cameo necklace with silver on onyx background, ca. 1970s. Silver metal frame, .88" x 1" and chain, 21" long. $95-125.

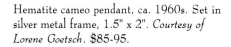

Hematite cameo pendant, ca. 1960s. Set in silver metal frame, 1.5" x 2". *Courtesy of Lorene Goetsch.* $85-95.

Left: Blue glass intaglio with flowers incised, ca. 1980s. Set in silver angular, twisted metal frame, 1.75" x 2". $45-55.
Right: Hematite cameo on onyx, ca. 1940s. Set in unusual rectangular silver metal frame, 1.25" x 1.5". $65-75.
The cameos in this photograph are *Courtesy of Lorene Goetsch.*

Left: Black onyx cameo brooch with portrait of woman, ca. 1890. Gold frame twisted, 1" x 1.25". $495-525.
Right: Black onyx brooch, ca. 1930s. Gold frame, 1.38" x 1.75". $400-500.
The cameos on this photograph are *Courtesy of Antiques By Daisy.*

Black onyx intaglio, ca. 1970s. Set in silver metal frame, 1.38" x 2". *Courtesy of Lorene Goetsch.* $125-150.

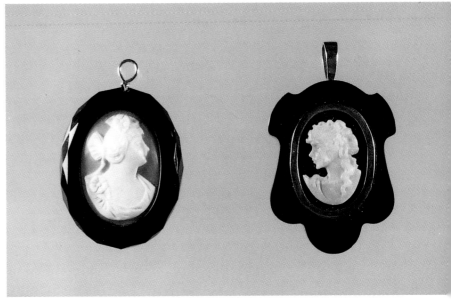

Left: Shell cameo pendant depicting woman with flower in hair and on shoulder, ca. 1880s. Cameo set in black onyx, gold bail, measures 1.3" x 1.75". $900-1200.
Right: Opal cameo pendant depicting portrait of woman, ca. 1880s. Set in black onyx frame with 14K gold, measures 1.38" x 1.8". $2500-3000.
The cameos in this photograph are *Courtesy of Frank and Dorothy Everts.*

Left: Black and white onyx brooch with portrait of woman in profile, ca. 1920s. Measures 1.62" x 2.12". *Courtesy of Mark's Collectibles.* $400-500.
Center: Small stone pendant of profile of woman, ca. 1890. Measures .4" x .62". *Courtesy of Bonnie Dupree.* $95-125.
Right: Glass pendant with portrait of woman, ca. 1930. Measures 1.25" x 1.75". *Courtesy of Mark's Collectibles.* $85-95.

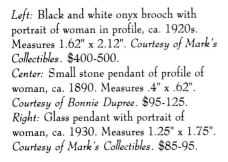

Top left: Onyx cameo brooch, ca. 1880. Hexagonal shape, 1.38" x 1.7" $150-225.
Top right: Signed Czechoslovakia obsidian cameo brooch, ca. 1875. Onyx backing, 1.25" x 1.62". $300-400.
Center: Celluloid cameo brooch, ca. 1880s. Profile of woman, 2." x 2.5". $125-150.
Bottom left: Onyx cameo pendant, ca. 1860s. Brass frame with gold and claw setting, 1.25" x 1.5". $165-235.
Bottom right: Celluloid brooch/pendant with profile of woman, ca. 1930. Sterling silver frame is hand-crafted, 1.5" x 1.75". *Courtesy of Mary Moon, Red Wagon Antiques.* $195-225.

Top left: Gold metal brooch in relief with profile of woman, ca.1890. Jet backing, 1.25" x 2". $150-175.
Top right: Onyx cameo brooch with white profile of woman on black, ca. 1890. Gold frame, 1.62" x 1.88". $500-600.
Center left: Onyx cameo locket/pendant, white on black, ca. 1860. Gold frame, 1.13" x 2.13". $500-600.
Center right: Onyx cameo locket/pendant, white on black, ca. 1860. Gold frame with seed pearls, 1.13" x 1.62". $550-650.
Bottom: Obsidian cameo on jet pendant, ca. 1890. Gold frame 2" x 3". $300-400.

Top: Shell cameo ring, ca. 1940s. Gold filled metal. *Courtesy of Lenora Alice Knighton.* $195-225.
Center: Onyx intaglio of helmeted figure on cuff links, ca. 1970s. Gold metal frame, .75" x .75". $125-175.
Bottom: Stone cameo earrings, ca. 1960s. Sterling backs with prongs, .5" x .75". $150-175.

Left: Shell cameo pendant depicting two seated figures of man and woman, ca. 1920s. Set in twisted wire frame, measures 1" in diameter. $400-500.
Top center: Stone cameo brooch depicting woman, ca. 1890s. Measures 1.12" x .38". $500-600.
Center: Stone cameo brooch, ca. 1880s. Elaborate frame with filigree and beading, measures 1.38" x .88". $600-800.
Bottom center: Bar pin with stone cameo depicting figure, ca. 1890s. Frame and pin have gold content, measures 2.75" x .62". $400-500.
Top right: Stone cameo pendant with drop stone, ca. 1900s. Measures .6" x .8". $900-1200.
Right: Stone cameo stickpin, ca. 1940s. Set in frame with etching and twisted wire, measures 2.75" x .62". $300-400.
The cameos in this photograph are *Courtesy of The Patrician Antiques.*

Top: High relief stone cameo depicting Demeter (Ceres), goddess of the harvest, ca. 1860. Etruscan style beading, pin has 10K gold frame, presentation box, .5" x .75". $400-500.
Bottom: Shell cameo pendant, ca. 1890. 14K gold frame, .75" x .88". $600-800.
The cameos in this photograph are *Courtesy of Carole Day.*

Red stone intaglio pendant with profile of woman in gold, ca. 1930s. Measures 1.12" x 1.5". *Courtesy of Lenora Alice Knighton.* $295-395.

Top left: One stone cameo cuff link depicting woman in profile, ca. 1940s. Measures .75" x 1.1". $225-275.
Top right: Fob stone intaglio with portrait of Classical figure, ca. 1890s. Set in frame with twisted wire, measures .75" x .75". $500-600.
Center: Celluloid set on glass cameo pendant of Psyche depicted with butterfly wing, ca. early 1900s. Set in gilt frame, measures 1.62" x 2". $250-350.
The cameos in this photograph are *Courtesy of George and Dotty Stringfield.*

Top: High relief stone cameo brooch, ca. 1890. Rose gold frame, .94" x 1.12". $500-600.
Bottom: Coral cameo necklace, ca. 1890. 14K gold frame with fresh water pearl, .5" x .75". $400-500.
The cameos in this photograph are *Courtesy of Florence B. Crank.*

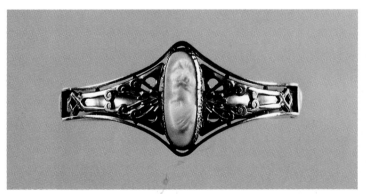

Signed stone cameo gold bracelet, ca. 1908. Cameo measures .38" x 1". *Courtesy of DeLorias Milam.* $1500-1800.

Chapter Three
Lava

Unless otherwise indicated the following lava cameos are ca. 1810-1860. *Courtesy of Frank and Dorothy Everts.*

High relief lava cameo with exquisite detail depicting Classical woman. Mounted on velvet in modern frame. Has slight damage to shoulder. $350-400.

Side view of portrait to show the high relief and carving. Mounted on velvet in modern frame, slight damage to shoulder.

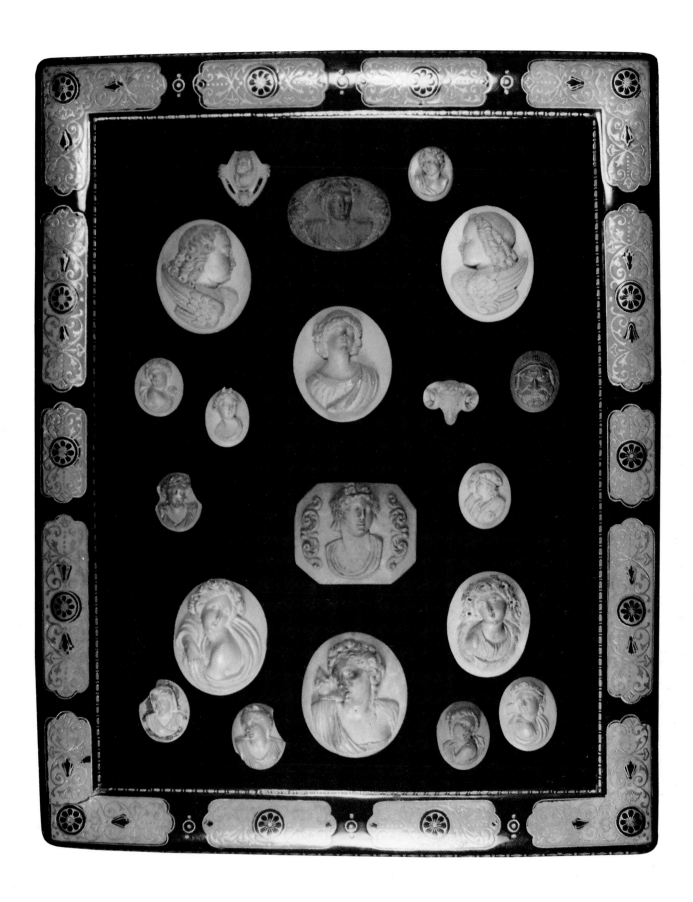

Twenty lava cameos of various colors depicting mythological motifs
and portraits. All cameos mounted on velvet in an Art Deco frame.

A variety of large and small lava cameos in various designs of
portraiture. Mounted on velvet in green Art Deco frame.

Lava carving in relief depicting religious figure. Mounted on velvet in modern frame. Has some damage to bottom center of carving and slight damage to nose. $195-225.

Side view of lava cameo to show relief of carving and detail. Set on red velvet background in modern frame.

High relief lava cameo carving of Classical woman. Mounted on red velvet background in modern frame. $275-295.

Lava cameo depicting Classical portrait of woman in relief. Mounted on velvet in modern frame. Has slight damage to right corner. $155-175.

Loose lava cameo in relief of religious figure. Mounted on velvet in modern frame, with some damage to lower right of carving. $195-225.

Lava cameo depicting mythological motif of Eros (Cupid), god of love, damage to top left of carving. Mounted on velvet in modern frame. $125-150.

Loose lava cameo in high relief depicting angel. Mounted on velvet in modern frame. $175-195.

Another view of angel in lava cameo to illustrate the depth and detail of carving. Mounted on velvet in modern frame.

Loose carved lava cameo of portrait in profile of bearded man. Mounted on velvet background in modern frame. $275-295.

High relief lava cameo depicting Classical woman wearing head ornament. Mounted on velvet in modern frame. $250-295.

Another view of lava cameo to illustrate the high relief and the intricate carving of the portrait. Mounted on velvet in modern frame.

Lava cameo in relief depicting the mythological portrait of Cronus (Saturn) with scythe, known as the god of agriculture. Mounted on velvet in modern frame. $295-325.

Another view of Cronus (Saturn) to illustrate the detail of the lava carving. Mounted on velvet in modern frame.

Hexagonal shaped lava cameo depicting portrait of Classical woman in relief. Mounted on velvet in modern frame. $125-150.

High relief carving depicting mythological motif of Bacchante maiden, follower of Dionysus (Bacchus) who was the god of wine and fertility. Mounted on velvet in modern frame. $350-395.

Side view of Bacchante maiden. Mounted on velvet in modern frame.

Lava cameo depicting mythological motif of Athena (Minerva), goddess of war, with an owl. Cameo mounted on velvet in modern frame, some damage to carving. $150-175.

High relief lava cameo depicting Eros (Cupid). Mounted on velvet in modern frame. $295-325.

Side view of Eros (Cupid) to show the intricate carving. Mounted on velvet in modern frame.

Unusually shaped lava cameo depicting muse. Mounted on velvet background in modern frame. $225-250.

Top: Lava cameo in relief depicting angel with wings. Mounted on velvet in modern frame. $125-150.
Bottom: Lava cameo in relief depicting portrait of Classical woman wearing head ornament. Mounted on velvet in modern frame. $145-150.

Lava cameo depicting mythological motif of Heracles, slayer of monsters, with bear and club. Mounted on velvet in modern frame, damage to cameo on lower right. $95-125.

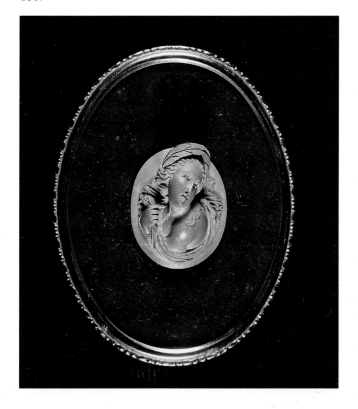

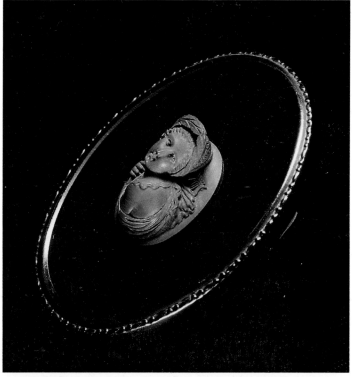

Loose lava cameo of muse in high relief. Mounted on velvet in modern frame. $375-395.

Another view of muse to show detail of carving. Mounted on velvet in modern frame.

Lava portrait in high relief depicting Eros (Cupid) with arrow. Mounted on velvet in modern frame. $275-295.

Side view of Eros (Cupid) to emphasize the detail of the carving. Mounted on velvet in modern frame.

Side view muse to emphasize the high relief and the intricate detail of facial features and curls in hair. Mounted on velvet in modern frame.

Lava cameo portrait of muse with lyre. Mounted on velvet in modern frame. $325-350.

Another view of portrait.

Lava cameo in high relief depicting Classical woman adorned with flowers in hair and on garment. Mounted on velvet in modern frame. $275-295.

Another view of muse. On velvet in modern frame.

Loose black lava cameo in relief depicting portrait of woman. On velvet in modern frame. $225-250.

Carved lava cameo depicting angel in profile
with wings and curls. On red velvet in
modern frame. $225-250.

Lava cameo in relief depicting religious figure in profile, on wooden
plaque. $275-295.

Loose lava cameo in high relief depicting Dionysus (Bacchus), god of
wine and fertility. On velvet in modern frame. $375-395.

Another view of Dionysus (Bacchus).
Mounted on velvet in modern frame.

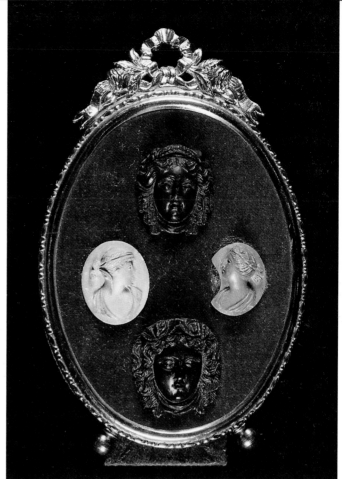

Black lava cameo portrait in profile of woman wearing head ornament. On velvet in modern frame, some damage to top left and bottom right of portrait. $125-150.

Black lava cameo in relief depicting portrait of Classical woman in profile. Mounted on velvet in modern frame, slight discoloration on left side of carving. $150-175.

Top: Black lava cameo of portrait in high relief. Mounted on velvet in modern frame. $145-165.
Center left: Lava cameo portrait of woman in profile. Set on velvet in modern frame, some damage to nose. $95-125.
Center right: Lava cameo depicting woman's portrait in relief, damage to left side of cameo. Set on velvet in modern frame, some damage to nose. $85-95.
Bottom: Black lava cameo depicting Classical portrait in high relief. Mounted on velvet in modern frame. $175-185.

Side view of portrait, mounted on velvet in modern frame. Slight discoloration on left side of carving.

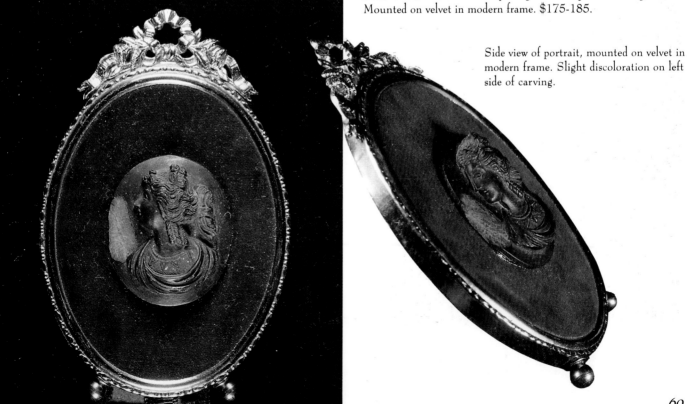

Lava cameo in relief depicting man's profile. Mounted on velvet in modern frame. $195-225.

Side view of man's portrait. Mounted on velvet in modern frame.

Black lava cameo depicting portrait in profile of man. Mounted on velvet in modern frame, damage to cameo on bottom right. $125-135.

Opposite page:

An assortment of cameos of various sizes depicting figures from mythology, angels, and portraits.

Top: Lava cameo bracelet with eight cameos depicting Classical portraits, ca. 1800s. $800-1200.

Center: Lava cameo earrings depicting mythological motif of Zeus, king of the gods, in chariot, measures .75" x .88", ca. 1800s. $450-650.

Bottom left: Lava brooch of Dionysus (Bacchus), god of wine and fertility, frame decorated with beads, acorns, and leaves, measures 1.62" x 1.8", ca. 1800s. $900-1200.

Bottom right: Lava brooch depicting mythological motif of Bacchante maiden, follower of Dionysus (Bacchus), god of wine and fertility, maiden has grapes and grape leaves in hair, frame with gold twisted wire, ca. 1800s. $600-800.

The cameos in this photograph are *Courtesy of Melissa A. Elrod.*

Top: Lava cameo earrings of women in profile, ca. 1860. Gold backs and frame with twisted wire, 1.25" x 1.5". $1200-1500.

Bottom: Lava cameo pendant depicting mythological motif of Psyche with butterfly wing, ca. 1850. Gold frame, .75" x 1.25". $600-800.

The cameos in this photograph are *Courtesy of Jackie McDonald.*

Bracelet with nine lava cameos of beige and green depicting Classical portraits, set in gold frames, with safety catch. *Courtesy of Frank and Dorothy Everts.* $900-1200.

Chapter Four
Shell

Shell with carving depicting mythological motif of Demeter (Ceres),
goddess of the harvest, with wheat in hair, ca. early 1900s. Measures
3.12" x 4.5". *Courtesy of The Patrician Antiques.* $700-1000.

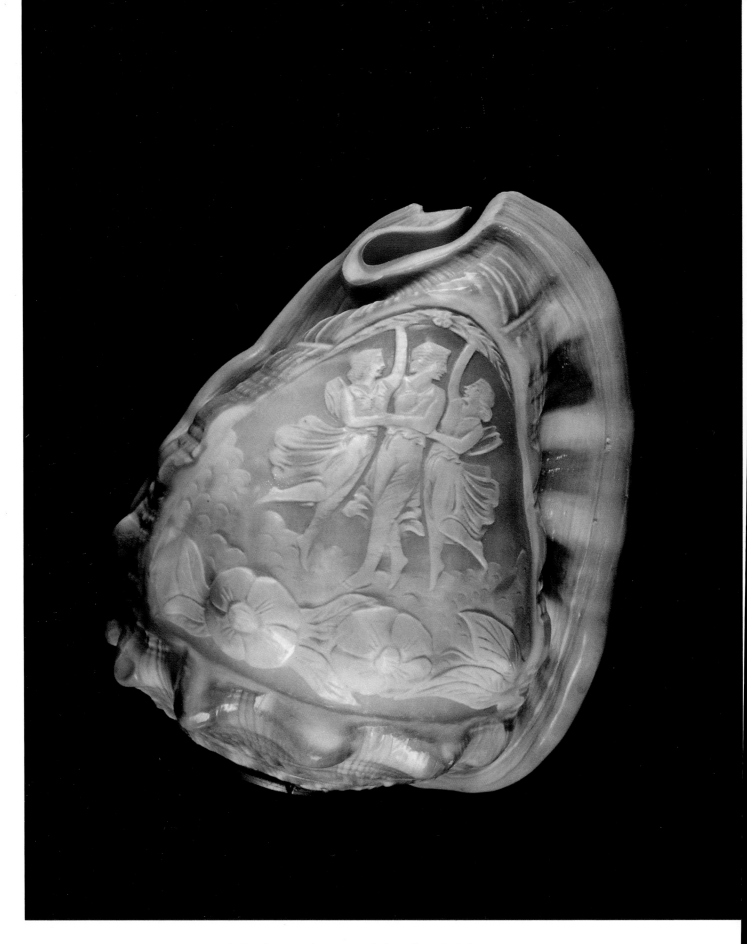

Shell with carving depicting mythological motif of Three Muses, ca.
1930s. *Courtesy of Frank and Dorothy Everts.* $800-1200.

Tiffany shell cameo brooch of two Roman figures, horse carved into helmet, spear and shield with winged figure in clouds, ca. 1890s. C clasp and Etruscan style beading, in gold frame, cameo came in presentation box, 2.25" x 2.75". *Courtesy of Melissa A. Elrod*. $5000-6000.

Top left: Shell cameo pendant of woman with flower in hair, ca. 1930s. Set in frame of twisted wire, measures .88" x 1.12". $300-400.

Center: Shell cameo brooch with mythological theme depicting Aphrodite (Venus) in shell rising from the sea with dolphins, ca. 1890s. Set in twisted wire frame, slight damage to left side background of cameo, measures 1.38" x 1.7" $600-800.

Top right: Shell cameo pendant depicting mythological motif of Psyche with butterfly wings, ca. 1890s. Set in sterling silver frame, measures 1" x 1.2". $300-400.

Bottom left: Shell pendant/locket of woman's portrait, ca. 1890s. Set in elaborate gold filled frame, measures 1" x 1.5". $400-500.

Bottom right: Shell cameo brooch of woman, ca. 1900s. Frame has safety catch, measures .88" x 1.2" $300-400.

The cameos in this photograph are *Courtesy of Melissa A. Elrod.*

Presentation box from Tiffany's.

Shell brooch/pendant with portrait of woman, ca. 1860. Frame decorated with gold leaves and acorns, measures 1.8" x 2.25". *Courtesy of Susie Squyres Rainey.* $950-1200.

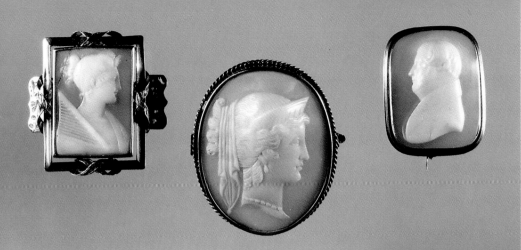

Left: Shell cameo brooch of woman's portrait, ca. early 1800s. Set in unusual square decorated frame of 14K gold, measures 1.50" x 1.50". $600-800.
Center: Shell cameo brooch depicting woman wearing jewelry and veil, ca. 1860s. Set in twisted wire frame of 10K gold, measures 1.5" x 1.88". $1500-2000.
Right: Shell cameo brooch depicting portrait of man, ca. early 1800s. Set in 18K gold frame, measures 1.12" x 1.38". $2000-3000.
The cameos in this photograph are *Courtesy of Frank and Dorothy Everts*.

Shell cameo depicting Eros (Cupid) with bow and arrows, ca. 1890s. Cameo mounted on plaque, cameo measures 1.5" x 1.88". *Courtesy of Kaye Cronk Ellison*. $600-800.

Top: Shell earrings of high relief of Roman woman, ca. 1890s. Measures .88" x 1.12". $200-300.
Center: Shell brooch/pendant of woman wearing head ornament and necklace, ca. 1840-1860. Set in 10K gold frame of twisted wire, 1.12" x 1.40". $450-550.
Bottom left: Shell cameo brooch depicting mythological motif of Bacchante maiden, a follower of Dionysus (Bacchus), god of wine and fertility, with wreath of grapes and grape leaves, ca. 1840-1860. Set in gold frame with Etruscan style beading, 1.62" x 2.12". $900-1200.
Bottom right: Shell cameo brooch of Classical figure in profile, ca. 1850. Set in gold frame with Etruscan style beading, 1.5" x 1.88". $600-800.
The cameos in this photograph are *Courtesy of Melissa A. Elrod*.

Top: Shell cameo of Classical woman with flowers in hair and on shoulder, ca. 1890s. No frame, 1.2" x 1.62". $300-500.

Center left: Shell cameo brooch depicting woman in profile wearing flowers and leaves in hair and on shoulder, ca. 1920s. Set in silver filigree frame, measures 1.5" x 1.75". $500-600.

Center right: Shell cameo brooch/pendant of profile of woman, ca. 1920s. Set in filigree and beaded frame, measures 1.38" x 1.75". $500-700.

Bottom: Shell cameo brooch of figure with curls and wreath of fruit and leaves in hair, ca. 1890s. Set in frame of twisted wire, measures 1.5" x 2". $900-1200.

The cameos in this photograph are *Courtesy of The Patrician Antiques.*

Top left: Shell cameo brooch with mythological motif depicting Artemis (Diana), goddess of the hunt, with crescent moon in her hair and bow and arrows behind her back, ca. 1930s. Set in gold filigree frame, 1.12" x 1.38". $600-900.

Top right: Shell cameo brooch of Classical figure in profile, ca. 1800s. Set in gold frame, 1" x 1.25". $400-600.

Center: Shell brooch depicting Classical woman, ca. 1850, measures .88" x 1.12". $350-450.

Bottom: Necklace with two agate drops, two matching shell cameos of woman's portrait, ca. 1920s. Twisted gold frames measure 1.3" x 1.7". Bottom cameo depicts mythological motif of Minerva (Athena), goddess of war, ca. 1890. Twisted gold frame measures .38" x .88". $1500-3000.

The cameos in this photograph are *Courtesy of Melissa A. Elrod.*

Left: Intricately carved shell cameo habillé brooch with diamond depicting mythological motif of Bacchante maiden, follower of Dionysus (Bacchus), god of wine and fertility, with wreath of grapes and leaves in hair, ca. 1860-1880. Set in gold frame with c clasp, 1.75" x 2.5". $1500-1800.

Right: Shell cameo pendant set in unusual 14K frame, depicts mythological motif of Diana (Artemis), goddess of the hunt, with crescent moon in hair and bow and arrows, ca. 1840. Gold frame, 1.12" x 2.62". $1500-1800.

The cameos in this photograph are *Courtesy of Melissa A. Elrod.*

Left: Shell cameo pendant with Roman warrior on horseback, ca. 1850. Set in twisted wire frame, 1.12" x 1.38". $600-800.

Center: Shell brooch of Classical figure in profile, ca. 1840. Ornate and unusual frame, 2.25" x 2.5. $1500-2000.

Right: Shell pendant of woman in profile wearing head ornament, ca. 1800s. Gold frame with twisted wire, 1.38" x 1.75". $300-500.

The cameos in this photograph are *Courtesy of Melissa A. Elrod.*

Left: Shell cameo brooch with flower motif, ca. 1860. Gold frame, 1.88" x 2.12". $495-550.

Right: Shell cameo brooch depicting mythological motif of Bacchante maiden, follower of Dionysus (Bacchus), god of wine and fertility, ca. 1850. Frame is unusual rectangular shape, 1.38" x 1.80". $550-600.

The cameos in this photograph are *Courtesy of Kathleen Cunningham.*

Left: Shell cameo portrait of woman, ca. 1860. Gold frame is 14K, 1.5" x 1.88". $600-700.
Right: Shell cameo portrait of woman, ca. 1915. Gold frame with twisted wire, 2" x 2.38". $400-500.
The cameos in this photograph are *Courtesy of Antiques By Daisy.*

Shell cameo earrings depicting scenes of Rebecca at the Well, ca. 1890. Gold metal with twisted effect and beading, .75" x 1". *Courtesy of Kaye Cronk Ellison.* $325-350.

Left: Shell cameo brooch/pendant featuring an unusual use of color in hair and garment is beautiful and intricately carved, ca. 1860. Frame is 14K gold, 1.38" x 1.8". $600-800.
Right: Shell cameo brooch/pendant of portrait in profile has some damage, ca. 1860. Gold frame measures 1.5" x 1.88. $250-275.
The cameos in this photograph are *Courtesy of Kathleen Cunningham.*

Top: Beautiful oval shell cameo pendant of village scene, ca. 1890s. Set in oval frame with beading and etching, measures 1.62" x 1.38". $600-700.

Bottom: Shell cameo depicting Angel of Death carrying two children with winged figure in the background, ca. 1890s. Set in oval frame with ribbon effect, measures 2.12" x 1.75" $1200-1500.

The cameos in this photograph are *Courtesy of The Patrician Antiques.*

Left: Shell cameo pendant depicting woman adorned with flowers in hair and on shoulder, ca. 1890s. Set in 14K gold frame of twisted wire, measures 1.5" x 1.88". $1500-2000.

Right: Shell cameo brooch/pendant depicting Demeter (Ceres), goddess of the harvest, with stalk of wheat, ca. 1930s. Set in twisted wire frame of 10K gold, measures 1.75" x 2.12". $600-700.

The cameos in this photograph are *Courtesy of Frank and Dorothy Everts.*

Top: Shell cameo brooch with portrait of religious figure, ca. 1880s. Set in ornate gold frame, 1.75" x 2". $700-800.

Center left: Shell cameo pendant with portrait of Victorian woman gazing at flower on shoulder, ca. 1870s. Set in filigree frame, 1.38" x 2.12". $600-800.

Center right: Shell cameo pendant depicting mythological motif of the birth of Athena (Minerva), goddess of war; her carved likeness springs from the head of her father, Zeus, ca. 1850s. Set in frame of twisted wire and filigree work, 1.2" x 1.75". $1500-2000.

Bottom: Shell cameo depicting mythological figure of Ares (Mars), god of war, who wears plumed helmet, ca. 1850s. Set in golden frame embossed with leaves and beads, measures 1.5" x 1.75". $400-600.

The cameos in this photograph are *Courtesy of The Patrician Antiques.*

Left: Pink shell cameo brooch of woman's portrait, ca. 1920s. Set in gold filled etched frame, measures 1" x 1.25". $300-400.
Top: Shell cameo brooch depicting portrait of anonymous woman, ca. 1890s. Set in frame of 10K gold, measures .75" x 1". $500-600.
Bottom: Pink shell cameo pendant depicting portrait of woman, ca. 1920s. Set in gold filled filigree frame, measures 1.25" x 1.5". $400-500.
Right: Shell cameo pendant of woman with flower on shoulder, ca. 1980s. Set in gold plated frame, measures 1" x 1.3". $300-500.
The cameos in this photograph are *Courtesy of Frank and Dorothy Everts.*

Top: Shell cameo brooch/pendant with floral motif, ca. 1880s. Gold frame with twisted wire, 1.12" in diameter. $400-500.
Center: Stone cameo brooch, ca. 1840. Gold frame, 2.4" x .75". $800-1000.
Bottom: Shell cameo brooch with hand holding flowers, ca. 1860s. Gold frame, measures 1.75" x 2". $475-600.

Shell cameo pendant with floral motif of flowers, ca. 1880s. Beaded pearl frame, 2.12" in diameter. *Courtesy of Melissa A. Elrod.* $425-595.

Top: Multi-colored shell brooch with floral motif, ca. 1920s. Measures 1.75" x 1.5". $300-500.
Center left: Shell brooch in unusual shape with floral motif, ca. 1880s. Set in gold frame, 1.25" x 1.45". $600-800.
Center right: Shell pendant/brooch with floral motif of carved roses, ca. 1890s. Set in beaded frame, 1.1" x 1.38". $400-500.
Bottom: Shell pendant/brooch with floral motif depicting bouquet of tulips, ca. 1880s. Set in gold frame, 1.5" x 1.88". $600-800.
The cameos in this photograph are *Courtesy of Melissa A. Elrod.*

Shell cameo depicting woman with butterfly on shoulder, flaw in shell used to depict sun, ca. 1840-60. Gold frame with leaves and vines in Victorian snake motif, 2" x 2.25. $1200-1500.

Shell cameo habillé brooch with mine cut diamonds in earrings and gold frame of twisted wire, mythological motif depicting Bacchante maiden, follower of Dionysus (Bacchus), god of wine and fertility, with wreath of grapes and grape leaves in hair, ca. early 1800s. Twisted gold frame, 2.25" x 2.62". *Courtesy of Melissa A. Elrod.* $900-1200.

Cameo pendant/brooch depicting the mythological motif of Dionysus (Bacchus), god of wine and fertility, with grape leaves in his hair, ca. 1850s. Set in octagonal etched frame, signed FP, measures 1.75" x 2.25". *Courtesy of Mary Pyland.* $1000-1500.

Top left: Shell cameo pendant of woman wearing flowers in hair, ca. 1890s. Set in 10K gold frame, measures 1.1" x 1". $500-700.

Top right: Shell brooch depicting mythological motif of Apollo with lyre, ca. 1890s. Measures .9" x 1.12". $300-500.

Bottom left: Shell cameo of woman with flowers on shoulder, ca. early 1900s. Set in 10K gold frame, measures 1.5" x 1.88". $400-600.

Bottom center: Shell cameo depicting woman with butterfly on shoulder, ca. 1920s. Frame with pearls, 1.12" x 1.38". $300-400.

Bottom right: Shell cameo depicting mythological motif of Demeter (Ceres), goddess of harvest and fertility, with stalk of wheat, ca. 1890s. Set in 14K gold frame, 1.38" x 1.75". $900-1200.

The cameos in this photograph are *Courtesy of Judith Ann Pharo.*

Top: Shell cameo pendant of woman's portrait, ca. 1940s. Gold frame, .62" x .75". Courtesy of *Yvette's Antiques.* $200-300.

Bottom: Shell cameo locket/brooch with c clasp depicting man and woman fishing, ca. 1850s. Gold frame, 1.25" x 1.5". $600-800.

Top: Shell cameo pendant depicting Eros (Cupid) with bow and arrows, ca. 1860s. Note the unusual use of shell to add color to hair, set in 18K gold, 1.5" x 1.88". $1200-1500.

Bottom: Shell cameo brooch depicting woman holding flowers, ca. 1880s. Note the use of shell to add color to wreath in hair, set in gold plated ornate frame, 1.75" x 2.25". $400-600.

The cameos in this photograph are *Courtesy of Frank and Dorothy Everts.*

Left: Shell cameo pendant with portrait of woman, ca. 1890s. Set in 14K gold frame, 1.25" x 1.75". $600-800.
Center: Shell cameo pendant depicting woman carrying basket of flowers, ca. 1950s. Set in 10K gold frame, 1.62" x 2.12". $400-600.
Right: Shell cameo pendant depicting woman adorned with flowers in hair and on shoulder, ca. 1860s. Set in 18K gold filigree frame, measures 1.5" x 1.75". $1200-1500.
The cameos in this photograph are *Courtesy of Frank and Dorothy Everts*.

Left: Shell brooch depicting a mythological motif of Persephone, ca. 1850. Set in a gold frame with turquoise and seed pearls, 1.88" x 2.12". $600-700.
Right: Shell pendant depicting cupids, ca. 1850. Set in a silver frame, 1.38" x 2.12". $600-800.
The cameos in this photograph are *Courtesy of Melissa A. Elrod*.

Top: Shell earrings, mythological motif of Hebe watering Zeus, ca. 1880s. Frame measures 1" x 1". $400-500.
Bottom: Shell cameo mourning brooch of Hebe watering Zeus, swivel locket, ca. 1880s. Frame is gold plate, 2.25" x 2.5". $1200-1500.
The cameos in this photograph are *Courtesy of Melissa A. Elrod*.

Shell cameo mounted on velvet in frame depicting scene with Aphrodite (Venus) and Cupids, ca. 1880s. Cameo measures 1.5" x 1.62". *Courtesy of Kaye Cronk Ellison.* $450-495.

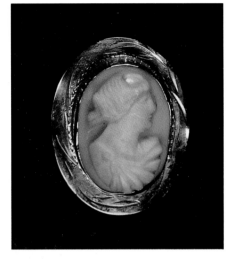

Shell cameo pendant, ca. 1800s. Frame 14K gold, .62" x 1". $850-1500.
Shell cameo carved with colored part of shell as hair, ca. 1800s. No frame, 1" x 1.5". $450-675.
The cameos in this photograph are *Courtesy of Lenora Alice Knighton.*

Shell cameo brooch of woman in profile, ca. 1870. Frame 10K gold, .75" x 1". *Courtesy of Emily Patterson Bonner.* $400-600.

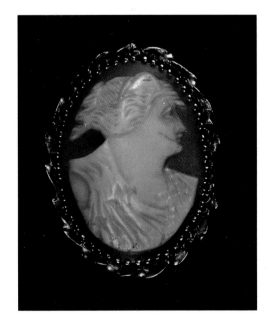

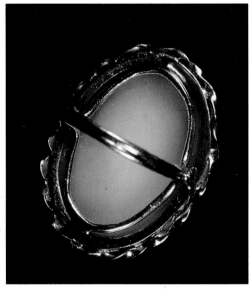

Shell cameo ring, ca. 1800s. Twisted 14K gold frame with beading, 1.33" x 1.75". *Courtesy of Judith M. Davis.* $500-800.

Shell cameo ring from reverse, ca. 1800s. Twisted 14K gold frame with beading, 1.33" x 1.75". *Courtesy of Judith M. Davis.* $500-800.

Top: Shell cameo brooch, ca. 1919. Frame gold wash over base metal, 1.38" x 2". $300-400.
Bottom left: Shell cameo pendant, ca. 1870. Frame gold wash over brass, 1.12" x 1.5". $400-500.
Bottom right: Shell cameo brooch/pendant in carved high relief, ca. 1900. Frame in 14K gold with turquoise stones and pearls, 1.38" x 2". $800-900.

Left: Signed shell cameo brooch/pendant with carved woman in medium relief, ca. 1950s. Gold frame is older and damaged, with seed pearls and aquamarine stones, 1.5" x 1.75". $350-450.
Right: Shell cameo habillé brooch/pendant of woman with flowers wearing diamond pendant, ca. 1915. White gold 14K frame, 1.5" x 2". $700-800.

Cameo bracelet depicting seven days from left to right: Monday: Artemis (Diana), goddess of the hunt, Tuesday: Ares (Mars), god of war, Wednesday: Hermes (Mercury), messenger for the gods, Thursday: Zeus (Jupiter), king of gods, Friday: Aphrodite (Venus), goddess of love, Saturday: Cronus (Saturn), god of agriculture, and Sunday: Apollo, god of music, ca. 1950s. Bracelet signed FP. $1400-1800.

Left: Shell cameo brooch/pendant depicting woman in profile wearing flower in hair, ca. 1890s. Frame and bail with garnets, safety clasp, 1.5" x 1.88". $1200-1500.
Right: Shell cameo brooch/pendant depicting mythological motif of Psyche with butterfly wings, ca. 1890. Set in filigree frame, 1.75" x 2.25". $900-1200.

Mother-of-pearl cameo bracelet with seven days of the week, ca. 1930s. Each cameo measures .5" x .75". $300-400.
Top left: Mother-of-pearl cameo pendant, ca. 1890. Gold metal frame has twisted wire, .88" x 1.12". $195-225.
Top right: Mother-of-pearl cameo pendant, ca. 1900. Gold metal frame with twisted wire, .75" x 1". $95-125.
The cameos in this photograph are *Courtesy of Shirley Falardeau.*

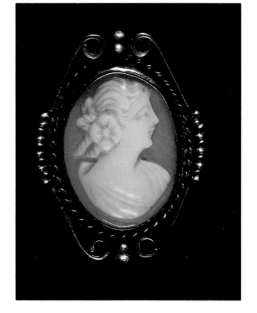

Shell cameo ring, ca. late 1800s. Silver metal, .75 x 1" on top. *Courtesy of Nana Dodds.* $150-300.

Shell cameo bracelet depicting seven days of the week, ca. 1930s. Sterling silver with twisted gold wire. *Courtesy of Nana Dodds.* $1500-1800.

Shell cameo ring of woman in profile, ca. 1930s. Ring is Italian silver with cameo measuring .5" x .62". *Courtesy of Frances L. McGinnis.* $200-300.

Shell cameo pendant, ca. 1890. Gold frame with garnets around cameo, 1.38" x 1.75", and garnet and gold necklace, 30" long. *Courtesy of Shirley Falardeau.* $700-900. .

Left: Shell cameo brooch depicting mythological motif of Psyche with butterfly wing, ca. 1915. Gold frame, 1.25" x 1.5". $500-600.
Right: Shell cameo habillé brooch of woman in profile with flowers in hair, ca. 1860. Gold frame, 1.38" x 1.75". Minor damage. $350-450.
The cameos in this photograph are *Courtesy of Kathleen Cunningham.*

Top left: Stone cameo brooch of Classical figure, set in unusual frame with c clasp, beads and embossed leaves, ca. 1870s. Measures .62" x .75", ca. 1870s. $300-400.

Top right: Shell pendant of woman's portrait, set in etched frame, ca. 1920s. Measures .6" x .7". $250-350.

Bottom left: Shell cameo brooch depicting mythological motif of Psyche with butterfly wing in hair, ca. 1890s. Set in gold frame of 10K gold, measures 1.25" x 1.5". $375-500.

Bottom center: Shell cameo brooch depicting mythological motif of Psyche with butterfly wings in hair and on shoulders, ca. 1900s. Set in beaded and etched frame of 10K gold, measures 1.5" x 1.88". $475-650.

Bottom right: Shell cameo brooch of woman's portrait in profile, ca. 1890s. Set in beaded and etched 10K gold frame with c clasp, measures 1.28" x 1.62". $425-550.

The cameos in this photograph are *Courtesy of Bobby and Mary Fyffe.*

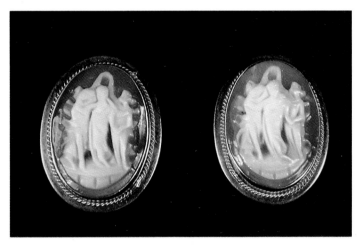

Shell cameo earrings portraying mythological motif of Three Muses, ca. 1800s. Gold frame has applied twisted wire, .38" x .5". *Courtesy of Garden Gate Antiques.* $300-400.

Left: Shell cameo brooch of woman with flower on shoulder, ca. 1930s. Set in ornate 10K gold frame of twisted ribbon and beaded wire, 1.3" x 1.6". $350-450.

Right: Shell cameo pendant depicting mythological motif of Artemis (Diana) with crescent moon, ca. 1890s. Set in octagonal shaped, gold plated, etched frame, 1.1" x 1.3". $375-475.

The cameos in this photograph are *Courtesy of River City Mercantile Cos., Jefferson, TX.*

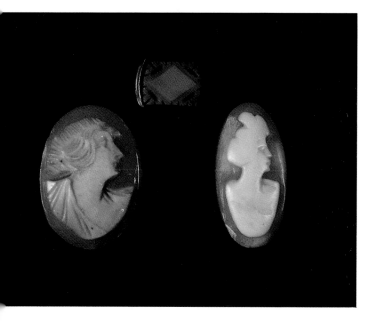

Left: Shell cameo with no frame, ca. 1915. Profile of a woman, .56" x .75". $300-400.
Center: Shell cameo from tie tack, ca. 1915. Yellow gold mounting, .25" x .38". $250-350.
Right: Shell cameo, ca. 1860. A typical ring setting, .31" x .75". $300-400.
The cameos in this photograph are *Courtesy of Garden Gate Antiques.*

Top left: High relief shell cameo of woman's portrait, ca. 1890s. Set in filigree frame, 1.2" x 1.4". $400-600.
Top right: Shell cameo depicting woman, ca. 1880s. Set in 10K gold beaded frame with Etruscan style beading, 1" x 1.38". $800-1200.
Bottom left: Shell cameo with portrait of woman, ca. 1890s. Set in 10K gold frame, 1.12" x 1.5". $800-1100.
Bottom right: Shell cameo of woman wearing jewelry, ca. 1920s. Set in 10K gold frame, 1.5" x 1.6". $900-1200.
The cameos in this photograph are *Courtesy of Judith Ann Pharo.*

Left top: Shell cameo habillé of woman wearing necklace with diamond, ca. 1920s. Set in filigree frame of 14K gold, 1.38" x 1.75". $900-1200.
Center: Shell cameo of woman wearing diadem, ca. 1920s. Set in 825 silver frame with marcasites, 1.62" x 2". $600-800.
Right: Shell cameo depicting woman wearing jewelry, ca. 1920s. Set in etched and Etruscan style beaded frame of 14K gold, 1.25" x 1.5". $1500-1800.
The cameos in this photograph are *Courtesy of Janet Johnson.*

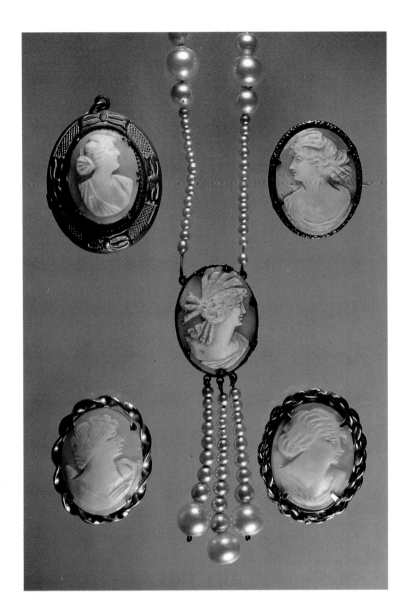

Top: Heart shaped shell cameo pendant/
locket, ca. 1890s. Measures .8" x .88".
$200-300.
Bottom: Shell cameo brooch/pendant
depicting woman holding bird, ca. 1920s.
Set in twisted frame, measures 2.1" x
2.62". $2000-3000.
The cameos in this photograph are *Courtesy
of Sandra F. Conn.*

Top left: Shell cameo pendant depicting Roman woman, ca. 1890s.
Set in beaded and decorated frame, 1.25" x 1.5". $600-800.
Top right: Shell cameo brooch depicting mythological motif of
Psyche with butterfly wing in hair, ca. 1890s. Set in distinctive
frame, 1" x 1.25". $700-900.
Center: Pearl necklace with shell cameo depicting woman's portrait,
ca. 1880s. Cameo measures .88" x 1.12", pearl dangles measure 2".
$1400-1600.
Bottom left: Shell cameo brooch of woman in profile, ca. 1890s. Set
in twisted wire frame, 1.12" x 1.38". $500-700.
Bottom right: Shell cameo brooch depicting portrait of woman, ca.
early 1900s. Set in twisted wire frame, 1.12" x 1.4". $400-500.
The cameos in this photograph *Courtesy of The Patrician Antiques.*

Shell cameo habillé depicting woman with
flowers on her shoulders wearing necklace,
ca. 1910. Set in filigree frame of 14K
white gold, 1.75" x 2.12". *Courtesy of
Frank and Dorothy Everts.* $1500-2000.

Left: Shell cameo pendant of woman with flowers in hair, ca. 1890s. Set in etched frame decorated with two silver knots, 1.62" x 2". $1200-1500.

Top: Shell cameo pendant of woman in profile, ca. 1890s. Set in frame with decorative beading and twisted wire, measures 1.38" x 1.75". $600-800.

Right: Shell cameo pendant of woman's portrait in profile, ca. 1920s. Set in decorated frame, 1.75" x 2.12". $1200-1500.

The cameos on this page are *Courtesy of The Patrician Antiques.*

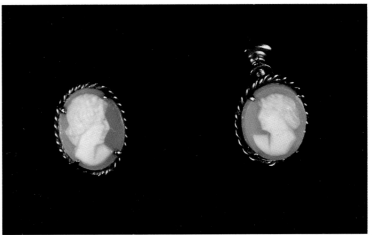

Two medium relief shell cameos set as earrings, ca. 1915. Twisted frames are 14K gold, .31" x .50". *Courtesy of Garden Gate Antiques.* $400-500.

Top: Shell cameo bracelet depicting woman in profile with flowers, ca. 1930s. Measures .88" in diameter. $400-500.

Center: Cuff cameo bracelet with shell cameo depicting woman with flowers on shoulder, ca. 1930s. Measures .75" x 1". $300-500.

Bottom: Gold cameo bracelet with shell cameo of woman's portrait set in beaded frame, ca. 1900. Measures 1.12" x 1.25". $1200-1500.

The cameo bracelets in this photograph are *Courtesy of Melissa A. Elrod.*

Left: Shell cameo habillé portrait of woman with flowers, ca. 1930s. Set in octagonal silver filigree frame, 1.12" x 1.62". $600-800.

Center: Shell cameo portrait of woman in profile with flower, ca. 1930s. Set in octagonal silver filigree frame with pearl beading, 1.38" x 1.88". $900-1200.

Right: Shell cameo portrait of woman with flower in hair and flower on shoulder, ca. 1940s. Set in heavy, ornate gold frame, 1.12" x 1.25". $700-900.

The cameos in this photograph are *Courtesy of Melissa A. Elrod.*

Left: Mother in old daguerreotype wears cameo shown at top right, ca. late 1800s.

Top right: Stone cameo brooch/pendant, ca. late 1800s. Gold frame, 1" x 1.25". $500-700.

Bottom right: Shell cameo brooch, ca. 1850. Gold frame, 1.25" x 1.5". $400-500.

The daguerreotype and the cameos in this photograph are *Courtesy of Carol Trigg.*

Left: Shell cameo brooch depicting the mythological motif of the Three Muses, ca. 1800s, measures 1.75" x 2.25". Note the use of shell to create color at top and bottom of carving. $900-1200.
Center: Shell cameo pendant of Three Muses, ca. late 1800s. Measures .8" x 1". Some damage to left side of frame. $300-400.
Right: Shell cameo brooch/pendant of Dionysus (Bacchus), god of wine and fertility, with grape leaves in hair, ca. 1890s. Set in ornate frame with acorns and beading, measures 1.88" x 2". $1200-1500.
The cameos in this photograph are *Courtesy of Melissa A. Elrod*.

The cameos in this photograph are *Courtesy of Antiques by Daisy*.
Left: Shell cameo brooch, reverse carved to leave color on top of piece for hair and earrings, ca. 1800s. Gold frame, 1.5" x 2". $1800-2500.
Top center: Shell cameo earrings, ca. 1915. Gold plated, .88" x 1.62". $150-200.
Bottom center: Shell cameo ring, ca. 1840-60. Gold, .75" x .88". $400-500.
Right: Shell cameo brooch/pendant, ca. 1940s. Gold frame is 14K, .88" x 1.62". $500-600.

Left: Signed shell cameo pendant depicting portrait in profile of woman with flowers in hair, ca. early 1800s. Coral set in frame at corners, measures 1.75" x 2.12". $2000-3000.

Right: Shell cameo brooch/pendant of woman with flowers in her hair and on shoulder, ca. 1880s. Unusually shaped, distinctive frame with filigree and twisted wire, measures 2" x 2.38". $3000-4000. The cameos in this photograph are *Courtesy of Melissa A. Elrod.*

Left: Cameo habillé brooch of woman in profile with flowers in hair and wearing dog collar choker, ca. 1920s. Set in silver frame of unusual shape, 1.62" x 1.88". $1500-2000.

Right: Shell brooch depicting mythological motif of Apollo playing the lyre, ca. 1890s. Ornate gold frame with gilt leaves, 1.65" x 1.75". $1500-2000.

The cameos in this photograph are *Courtesy of Melissa A. Elrod.*

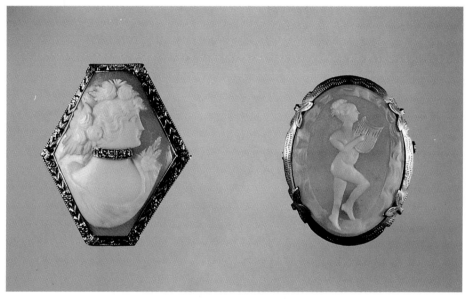

Top: Shell cameo brooch of Francis of Assisi with bird in left hand, ca. 1915. Frame of filigree and twisted wire decorated with flowers and leaves at corners, measures 1.25" x 1.5". $2000-3000.

Bottom left: Shell cameo brooch/pendant with religious motif of Madonna, ca. 1915. Set in twisted wire frame, measures 1.62" x 2.12". $1500-2500.

Bottom right: Rectangular shell cameo of woman's portrait with flowers, ca. 1930. Silver frame of filigree and decorated with flowers, measures 1.88" x 2.12". $1500-2500.

The cameos in this photograph are *Courtesy of Melissa A. Elrod.*

Left: Signed shell cameo brooch/pendant with two faces, ca. 1930. Frame is 14K gold with Etruscan style beading, 1.5" x 1". $900-1200.
Right: Signed shell cameo brooch/pendant with Three Muses, ca. 1910. Frame 14K gold with Etruscan style beading, 1" x 1.25". $1200-1500.
The cameos in this photograph are *Courtesy of Lenora Alice Knighton.*

Shell cameo bracelet with portrait of woman in profile, ca. 1920s. Cameo measures .75" x 1". *Courtesy of Donna Hanner.* $600-750.

Top: Shell cameo brooch depicting mythological motif of Dionysus (Bacchus), god of wine and fertility, ca. 1860. Gold frame decorated with twisted wire and seed pearls, 1.66" x 1.75". $300-400.
Bottom left: Shell cameo brooch/pendant, ca. 1915. Frame 14K gold, 1.25" x 1.5". $900-1200.
Bottom right: Shell floral cameo brooch/pendant, ca. 1890. Gold frame has twisted wire, 1.25" x 1.66". $600-800.
The cameos in this photograph are *Courtesy of Jackie McDonald.*

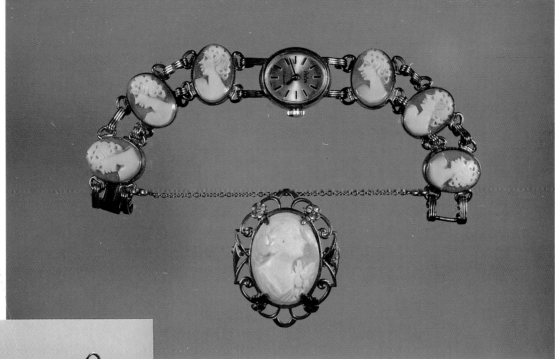

Pedro 17 jewel watch with six shell cameos with woman's portrait on band, 1/120 12KGF band, ca. 1950s. *Courtesy of Patricia Farren.* $300-400.
Bottom: Shell brooch/pendant of woman's portrait, ca. 1920s. Set in frame decorated with gold leaves. $300-400.

Top: Plastic cameo brooch of woman's portrait, ca. 1960s. Set in twisted wire frame, measures .75" x 1". $65-85.
Bottom: Bracelet, with seven shell cameos depicting woman's portrait, slight damage to one cameo, ca. 1950s. Set in frames of twisted wire, each cameo measures .62" x .75". *Courtesy of Margie M. Sparks.* $700-900.

Top left: Shell cameo brooch depicting Medusa, ca. 1890s. Set in gold frame, .8" x 1". $300-400.
Top right: Shell brooch/pendant of woman, ca. 1920s. Set in frame of 14K gold, Bartoli & Russo, Naples, Italy, measures 1" x 1.25". $500-750.
Bottom: Florenza shell brooch/pendant depicting portrait of a woman in profile with stone drop, measures 1.3" x 2.38", ca. 1950s. $200-300.
The cameos in this photograph are *Courtesy of Donna Harp Head.*

Top left: Shell cameo brooch of woman with upswept hair, ca. early 1900s. Set in gold frame with twisted wire, .88" x 1.12". $500-600.

Top right: Shell cameo pendant, portrait of woman with flower on shoulder, ca. 1920s. Set in twisted wire frame, .75" x 1". $500-600.

Center: Shell cameo brooch of Classical figure, ca. 1890s. Unusual frame with twisted wire is beaded with colorful stones, 1.38" x 1.3". $1500-2000.

Bottom left: Shell cameo brooch of woman in profile adorned with flowers, ca. 1930s. Set in twisted wire frame, 1" x 1.25". $400-600.

Bottom right: Shell cameo brooch/pendant of woman's portrait, ca. 1920s. Set in frame of twisted wire, 1" x 1.25". $300-500.

The cameos in this photograph are *Courtesy of The Patrician Antiques.*

Top: Shell cameo depicting chariot driver and horses, ca. 1880. No frame, 1.6" x 1.3". $300-400.

Bottom left: Shell cameo of woman's profile, ca. 1930s. No frame, 1.5" x 1.62". $250-350.

Bottom right: Loose shell cameo of woman with flowers on shoulder, ca. 1920s. Measures 1.1" x 1.38". $200-300.

The cameos in this photograph are *Courtesy of Frank and Dorothy Everts.*

Left: Shell cameo locket/pendant depicting portrait of woman, ca. 1850s. Set in frame with etching and beaded edges, 1.25" x 1.5". $900-1200.

Center: Shell cameo pendant, set in twisted wire frame, ca. 1930s. Gold frame measures 1.12" x 1.38". $700-900.

Right: Florenza shell cameo of woman with flower in hair, ca. 1940s. Set in frame with pearls, 1.38" x 1.75". $200-300.

The cameos in this photograph are *Courtesy of The Patrician Antiques.*

Signed shell bracelet with six cameos, ca. 1890. Gold with twisted frames, each cameo measures .6" x .75" and bracelet measures 7.5" long. $1500-2000.
Signed cameo earrings, ca. 1930s. Gold is 1.120 12K GF, .88" x 1". $400-500.
The cameos in this photograph are *Courtesy of Sue Rainey Pruitt.*

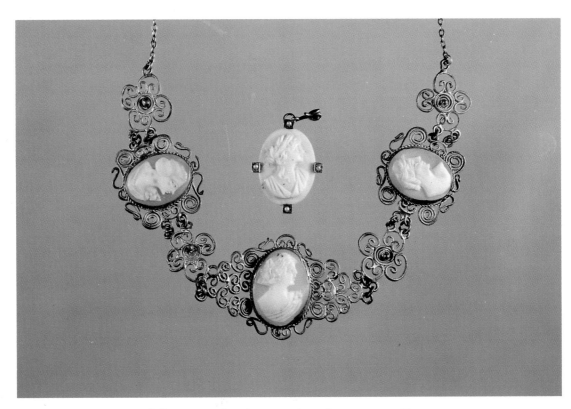

Top: Shell cameo pendant depicting Classical woman in profile, ca. 1860. Gold metal, measures .75" x 1". 400-500.
Bottom: Shell cameo necklace with three different profiles of woman's portrait, ca. early 1900s. Gold necklace with one cameo measuring .88" x 1.12" and other two are .88" x .88". $1500-2500.
The cameos in this photograph are *Courtesy of Kathleen Cunningham.*

Top left: Shell cameo pendant of woman with flower on shoulder, ca. 1890s. Set in frame with twisted wire, measures 1.3" x 1.7". $400-500.

Top right: Shell cameo brooch of woman's portrait, ca. 1890s. Set in frame with Etruscan style beading, measures 1.2" x 1.5". $500-600.

Bottom: Florenza shell cameo pendant necklace, ca. 1940s. Measures 1.5" x 1.75". $200-300.

The cameos in this photograph are *Courtesy of The Patrician Antiques.*

Top: Shell cameo brooch/pendant of woman in profile, ca. 1900. Set in gold metal frame, measures 1" x 1.25". $500-600.

Center left: Shell pendant depicting portrait of woman with flower on her shoulder, ca. 1920s. Set in gold frame with rhinestones and pearls, measures 1.25" x 1.5". $700-900.

Center right: Celluloid cameo portrait with mythological motif of Hermes (Mercury) with wings on hat, ca. 1890. Gold frame 1.38" in diameter. $200-300.

Bottom: Mother-of-pearl cameo with portrait of woman, ca. 1900. Gold frame, measures 1.12" x 1.88". $250-350.

The cameos in this photograph are *Courtesy of Melissa A. Elrod.*

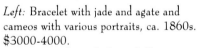

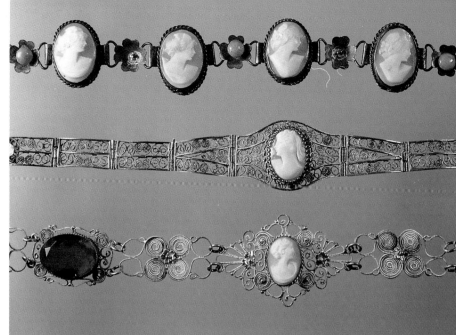

Top: Bracelet with coral beads (one missing) and shell cameos, cameos ca. 1920s. Set in twisted wire frames, each cameo measures .6" x .7". $1200-1500.

Center: Shell cameo bracelet with filigree and portrait of woman in profile ca. 1890s. Set in frame with beading and twisted wire on gold bracelet, cameo measures .5" x .62". $900-1200.

Bottom: Cameo of woman on bracelet, ca. early 1900s. Twisted wire and beading along with red stones, cameo measures .38" x .5". $1500-2000.

The cameo bracelets in this photograph are *Courtesy of The Patrician Antiques*.

Left: Bracelet with jade and agate and cameos with various portraits, ca. 1860s. $3000-4000.

Center: Bracelet with three shell cameos depicting portraits of women, ca. 1940s. Set in twisted wire frames in bracelet with filigree. $1500-2500.

Right: Shell cameo earrings depicting women in profile, ca. 1930s. Set in octagonal frames, measure 1" x 1.25". $400-500.

The cameo jewelry in this photograph is *Courtesy of Melissa A. Elrod*.

Shell cameo pendant depicting woman with flower in hair and on shoulder, cameo has some damage, ca. 1916. Gold wash over base metal frame, 1.5" x 1.75". *Courtesy of Marianne Mason.* $150-250 as is.

Left: Shell cameo pendant, ca. early 1900s. Unique gold frame with cupids, 1.12" x 1.25". $300-400.

Center: Shell cameo pendant with profile of woman with flower in her hair, ca. early 1900s. Gold frame, 1.12" x 1.66". $350-450.

Right: Florenza shell cameo of woman with flower in hair, ca. 1940s, set in frame with pearls, measures 1.38" x 1.66". $150-200. The cameos in this photograph are *Courtesy of Mary Sax.*

Left: Shell cameo brooch/pendant of woman in profile with flower in hair and on shoulder, ca. 1920s. Frame is 1/20 12K gold, 1.12" x 1.3". $375-450.

Right: Shell cameo brooch/pendant depicting woman's profile, ca. 1890s. Set in frame with coiled wire, measures 1.12" x 1.3". $200-300.

The cameos in this photograph are *Courtesy of George and Dotty Stringfield.*

Signed Florenza shell cameo brooch, ca. 1950s. Gold metal frame designed with twists and beads, 1.5" x 1.62". *Courtesy of Judith M. Davis.* $125-200.

Shell cameo brooch/pendant, ca. 1930s. Sterling silver frame signed 925, 1.5" x 1.88". *Courtesy of Judith E. Williams.* $400-500.

Shell cameo custom carved with portrait,
ca. 1940s. Frame has marcasites, 1.62" x
2". *Courtesy of Patsy W. Poulos.* $1200-
1500.

Shell cameo brooch with portrait of woman,
ca. 1930. Unusual gold frame, 1.12" x
1.3". *Courtesy of DeLorias Milam.* $325-
450.

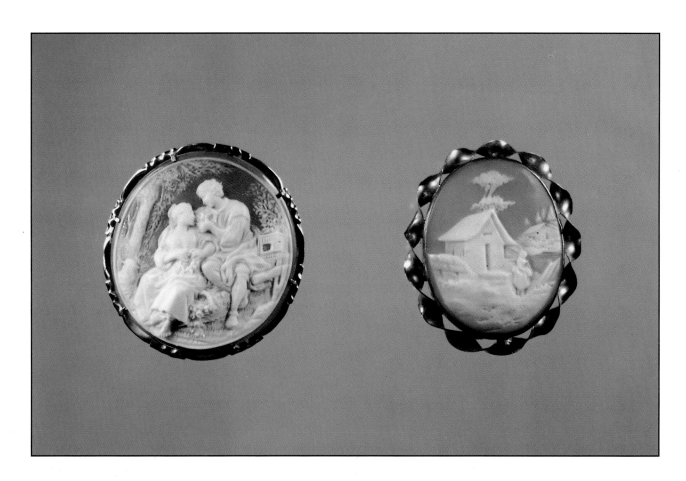

Left: Shell cameo brooch signed APA with scene from Pastorale by
Bouche from the original painting at the Louvre Museum, Paris,
France, ca. 1977. Frame is 14K gold, 2" in diameter. $2500-3500.
Right: Shell cameo brooch depicting Rebecca At Well, ca. 1860.
Gold frame, 1.75" x 2". $1200-1500.
The cameos in this photograph are *Courtesy of DeLorias Milam.*

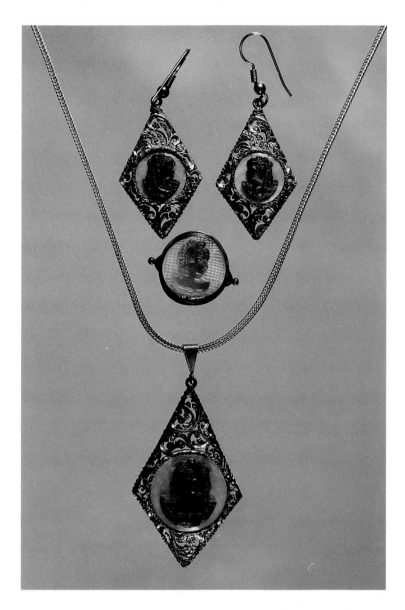

Mother-of-pearl cameo necklace with Etruscan beading, ca. 1930s. Gold frame, .62" x .75". *Courtesy of Cindy Porter.* $200-300.

Top: Jet cameo earrings with portrait of woman, ca. 1890s. Set in mother-of-pearl background with vermeil frames, .88" x 1.5". $250-350.
Center: Ring depicting woman in profile, ca. 1890s. Set in mother-of-pearl, frame is silver, .75" in diameter. $150-250.
Bottom: Jet necklace with cameo of woman on mother-of-pearl, ca. 1890s. Set in vermeil frame, measures 1.12" x 2" in diameter. $325-450.
The cameos in this photograph are *Courtesy of Melissa A. Elrod.*

Mother-of-pearl cameo bracelet and pendant cameos, ca. 1890. Silver plate metal work on both pieces. *Courtesy of Lenora Alice Knighton.* $800-1500.

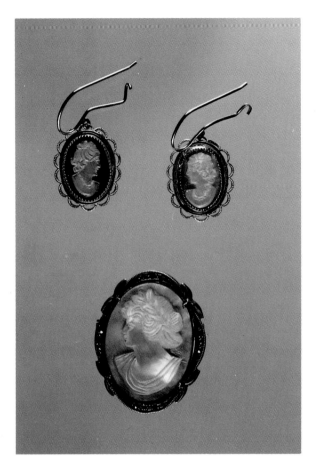

Top: Shell earring with profile of woman with curls, ca. 1920s. Frame is twisted wire, .62" x .75". $200-300 for pair.
Left and right: Florenza earrings of shell depicting woman in profile, ca. 1940s. With pearls in frame, measures 1" x 1.12". $225-275.
Bottom: Shell cameo of woman with flowers in her hair, ca. 1940s. No frame, measures .75" x 1". $150-250.
The cameos in this photograph are *Courtesy of George and Dotty Stringfield.*

Mother-of-pearl cameo brooch/pendant, ca. 1930s. Sterling silver frame, 1" x 1.38". $250-350.
Mother-of-pearl cameo earrings, ca. 1930s. Sterling silver frame, .42" x .62". $200-300.
The cameos in this photograph are *Courtesy of Shirley Falardeau.*

Life size illustration of loose shell cameos depicting various portraits of generalized women, ca. 1890s-1920s. Cameos range in price from $45-85.
Center: Shell cameo pendant depicting mythological motif of muse, ca. 1880s. No frame, measures .5" x 1". $200-300.
The cameos in this photograph are *Courtesy of Ollie Mae Waren.*

Shell cameo brooch/pendant of woman's portrait, ca. 1920s. Set in frame of 14K gold, measures .8" x 1". $400-600.
The cameo in this photograph is *Courtesy of Darlene Irwin*.

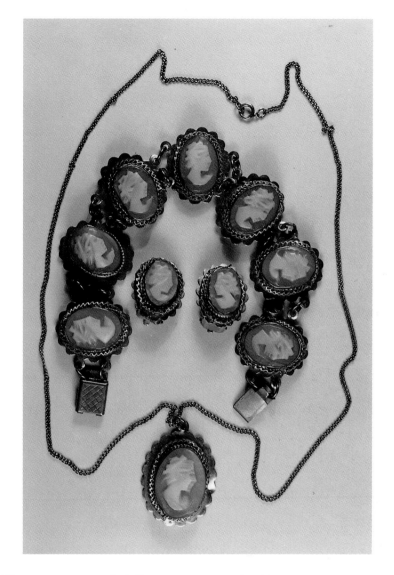

Demi-parure with shell cameos consisting of necklace, earrings, and bracelet, ca. late 1930s. Gilt over silver with twisted wire. *Courtesy of Nana Dodds*. $1000-1500.

Signed shell cameo bracelet with six cameos, ca. 1860. Gold metal with twisted rope design. $400-450.
Shell cameo brooch depicting mythological motif of Dionysus (Bacchus), god of wine and fertility, ca. 1860. Gold frame decorated with twisted wire and seed pearls, 1.66" x 1.75". $300-400.
The cameos in this photograph are *Courtesy of Great Finds & Designs, Inc. of Texarkana*.

Shell cameo brooch/pendant of woman in profile with flower on shoulder, ca. 1900s. Frame 14K gold. 1.62" x 1.38". *Courtesy of Mansion on Main Bed and Breakfast*. $400-450.

Shell brooch and earring set, ca. 1930s. Gold frame with pearls, brooch measures 1" x 1.38" and earrings measure .62" x .75". *Courtesy of Shirley Falardeau*. $500-650 for set.

Top: Sarah Coventry ring of woman facing right, mother-of-pearl, ca. 1960s. Measures .5" x .8". $150-250.
Bottom: Mother-of-pearl brooch/pendant of woman, ca. 1960s. Measures 1.1" x 1.25". $200-300.
The cameos in this photograph are *Courtesy of Mark's Collectibles*.

Left: Mother-of-pearl cameo ring, ca. 1900. Sterling silver. $225-300.
Center left: Shell cameo ring, ca. 1915. Sterling silver. $250-325.
Center: Shell cameo ring, ca. 1930s. Sterling silver. $225-325.
Center right: Shell cameo ring, ca. 1930s. Sterling silver. $195-250.
Right: Shell cameo ring, ca. 1950s. Gold tone. $125-200.
The cameos in this photograph are *Courtesy of Shirley Falardeau*.

Left: Shell cameo locket/pendant, ca. 1930s. Frame 12KGF, 1" x 1.25". *Courtesy of Gold Leaf Antiques.* $325-400.
Center: Shell cameo pendant signed 1947, Made In Italy. Gold frame has twisted wire, .5" x .62". *Courtesy of Cindy Porter.* $425-550.
Right: Signed shell cameo brooch/pendant, ca. 1930s. Gold frame, 1" x 1.25". *Courtesy of Cindy Porter.* $350-400.

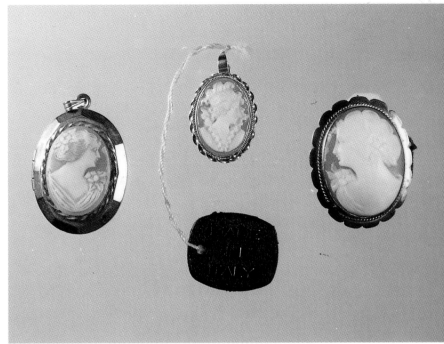

Shell cameo necklace, ca. 1915. Gold metal necklace with cameo measuring .62" x .75". *Courtesy of Shirley Falardeau.* $225-300.

Left: Shell cameo brooch, ca. 1930s. Gold frame with pearls, 1.25" x 1.5". *Courtesy of Ruby B. Stroud.* $300-400.
Center: Shell cameo brooch, ca. 1915. Silver frame with gold Etruscan style beading, 1.2" x 1.62". *Courtesy of Margaret McRaney.* $300-400.
Right: Shell cameo brooch, ca. 1915. Gold frame, 1.25" x 1.5". *Courtesy of Margaret McRaney.* $300-400.

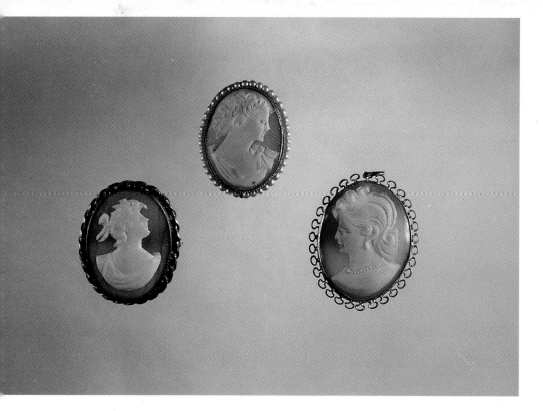

Left: Shell cameo brooch depicting Classical woman in profile, ca. 1890. Twisted gold frame, 1.12" x 1.38". $300-400.
Center: Shell brooch/pendant with profile of woman with flower in hair and on shoulder, ca. 1930s. Gold frame with pearls, 1" x 1.25". $300-400.
Right: Shell brooch/pendant depicting modern woman, ca. 1940s. Gold frame, 1.2" x 1.5". $350-500.
The cameos in this photograph are *Courtesy of Kathleen Cunningham.*

Top left: Shell pendant of woman in profile with flowers in hair, ca. 1930s. Frame sterling silver, 1.12" x 1.38". $450-550.
Top right: Shell brooch/pendant of woman's portrait, ca. 1950s. Frame 14K gold, .88" x 1.12". $325-400.
Center: Shell brooch depicting woman in profile, ca. 1930s. Gold frame damaged, 1.25" x 1.5". $225-250.
Bottom left: Shell pendant of woman adorned with flowers in hair and on shoulder, ca. 1930. Frame gold with pearls, 1" x 1.25". $400-600.
Bottom right: Signed shell brooch/pendant with portrait of woman with flowers in hair and on shoulder, ca. 1930s. Gold frame, 1.12" x 1.4". $400-600.
The cameos in this photograph are *Courtesy of Kathleen Cunningham.*

Shell pendant/brooch of woman, ca. 1915. Set in ornate gold frame with safety catch, 1.25" x 1.5". *Courtesy of Virginia Giles.* $400-500.
Right: Shell cameo brooch depicting mythological motif of Artemis (Diana), goddess of the hunt, with crescent moon in hair, ca. 1850. Set in gold frame. $250-300.

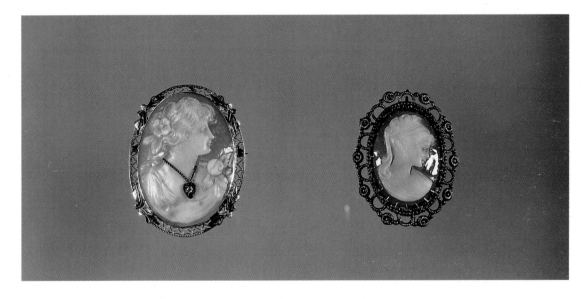

Left: Shell cameo habillé with diamond, depicts woman with flowers in her hair and a flower on shoulder, ca. 1915. Silver filigree frame with leaves at corners, 1.25" x 1.62". *Courtesy of Tracy Rothermel.* $600-700.
Right: Signed shell cameo pendant/brooch of woman, ca. 1920. Gold frame with beading, new safety catch added, 1.12" x 1.4". *Courtesy of June Owen.* $400-600.

Shell cameo brooch, ca. early 1900s. Frame is gold with a twisted ribbon effect, 1.25" x 1.5". *Courtesy of Lillian R. McClerkin.* $400-500.

Shell cameo brooch/pendant of woman with flower, ca. 1950s. Frame is 14K gold, .88" x 1.12". *Courtesy of Lauren Remica Gray*. $350-425.

Top: One shell earring with clip on back, ca. 1930s. Frame gold metal, .75" x 1". $135-165 for pair.
Bottom: Shell clip on earrings, ca. 1980s. Gold frame with twisted wire, .88" x 1". $250-325.
The cameos in this photograph are *Courtesy of Kathleen Cunningham*.

Shell cameo earrings of woman in profile, ca. 1915. Frame 12K gold filled. $200-300.
Shell cameo brooch/pendant depicting woman in profile with flower in hair, ca. 1915. Frame 14K gold. $400-600.
Shell cameo bracelet, ca. 1915. Gold metal. $225-300.
The cameos in this photograph are *Courtesy of Great Finds & Designs, Inc. of Texarkana*.

Shell cameo of woman in profile, ca. 1890s. Set in ornate frame, cameo measures 1.25" x 1.62". *Courtesy of Frank and Dorothy Everts*. $900-1200.

Top left: Shell cameo earring, ca. 1940s. Gold frame, .38" x .5". $95-150.
Top right: Shell cameo earring, ca. 1930s. Gold frame, .38" x .4". $150-175.
Center: Shell cameo earrings, ca. 1950s. Gold frame, .5" x .65". $200-300.
Bottom: Florenza signed shell earrings, ca. 1950s. Gold and pearl frame, 1" x 1.5". $150-225.
The cameos in this photograph are *Courtesy of Antiques By Daisy*.

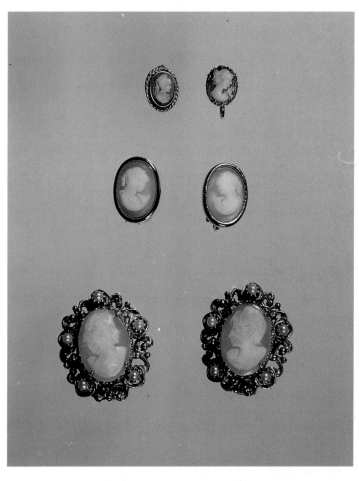

Left: Shell cameo brooch with profile of woman, ca. 1930s. Frame is 14K gold, 1.25" x 1.25". $700-900.
Right: Shell cameo brooch with profile of woman, ca. 1960s. Gold frame, 1.38" x 1.75". $400-500.
The cameos in this photograph are *Courtesy of Jane Qualls*.

113

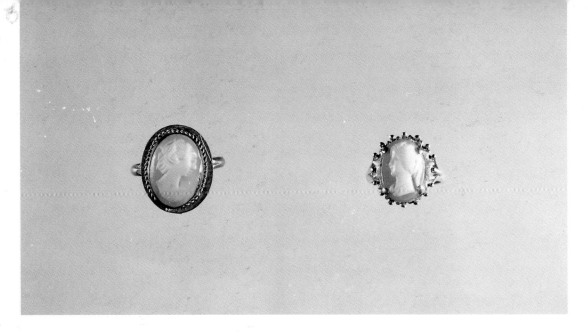

Left: Shell cameo ring of anonymous woman set in braided frame, ca. 1930s. 925 Sterling silver. $150-225.
Right: Shell cameo ring of woman wearing necklace, ca. 1930s. Frame is 10K RG. $225-295.
The cameos in this photograph are *Courtesy of Kathleen Cunningham.*

Shell cameo brooch/pendant, ca. 1940. 14K gold frame, .75" x .88". *Courtesy of Carol Trigg.* $300-400.

Top left: Signed shell cameo earrings, ca. 1930s. Frame 1/120 12K GF, .38" x .45". $150-225.
Top right: Shell cameo stick pin, ca. 1980. Gold metal, .25" x .3". $75-95.
Center: Shell cameo ring, ca. 1930s. Gold metal, .25" x .3". $225-250.
Bottom: Glass cameo earrings, ca. 1950s. Gold frame, .75" in diameter. $85-125.
The cameos in this photograph are *Courtesy of Mary Sax.*

Shell cameo pendant/brooch of woman adorned with flowers in hair and on shoulder, ca. 1920s. Set in 14K gold frame of twisted and beaded wire, measures 1" x 1.25". *Courtesy of Helen Lewis.* $600-800.

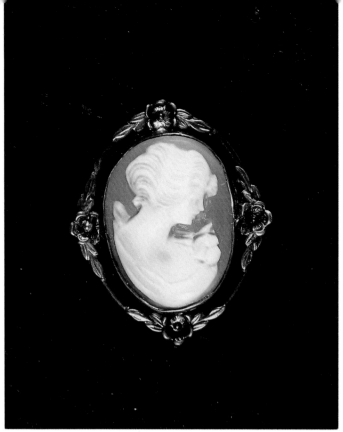

Shell cameo brooch of woman in profile with flower on shoulder, ca. 1930. Frame 1/20 12K gold, 1.25" x 1.5". *Courtesy of Nell Palmer Orr.* $400-600.

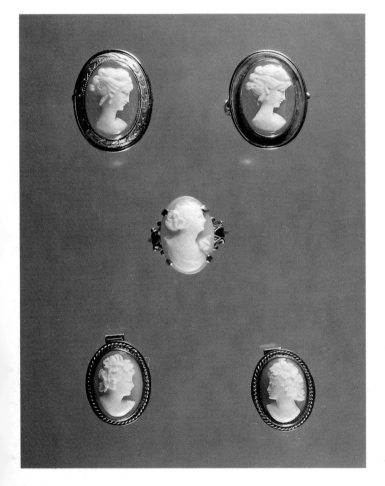

Top left: Ring, shell cameo with woman's portrait, ca. 1900. 14K gold, .88" x 1". *Courtesy of Maureen Gallagher.* $400-600.
Top right: Ring, shell cameo portrait of woman, ca. 1900. 14K gold, .88" x 1". *Courtesy of Maureen Gallagher.* $400-600.
Center: Shell ring of woman with flowers in her hair and on shoulder, ca. 1930s. 14K gold, .75" x .88". *Courtesy of Mark's Collectibles.* $350-450.
Bottom: Shell cameo cuff links, mythological motif of Bacchante maiden, follower of Dionysus (Bacchus) with grapes and grape leaves in her hair, ca. 1890s. Frames of twisted wire, .7" x .88". *Courtesy of Sue Rainey Pruitt.* $350-425.

Back of shell cameo brooch, ca. 1930. Frame 1/20 12K gold, 1.25" x 1.5". *Courtesy of Nell Palmer Orr.* $400-600.

Signed shell cameo brooch/pendant purchased in Italy, ca. 1980s. Frame 14K gold, has twisted wire around cameo, .88" x 1". $325-425.

Back of signed shell cameo brooch/pendant purchased in Italy, ca. 1980s. Frame 14K gold, has twisted wire around cameo, .88" x 1". $325-425.

Signed shell cameo brooch/pendant with two faces, ca. 1960. Gold frame with twisted wire, 1.33" x 1.67". *Courtesy of Garden Gate Antiques*. $600-800.

Top: Shell cameo ring, ca. early 1900s. Ring reset in 1970s, 10K gold. $225-275.
Bottom left: Shell cameo ring, ca. early 1900s. Reset in 1970s, 12K gold filled. $325-395.
Bottom right: Shell cameo necklace, ca. 1970s. $325-395.
The cameos in this photograph are *Courtesy of Lenora Alice Knighton*.

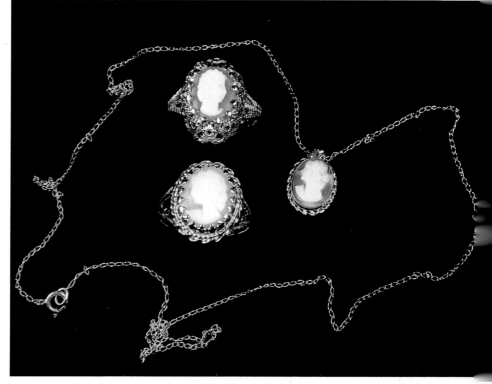

Top left: Shell cameo pendant with woman in profile, ca. 1930s. Set in gold frame, 1.12" x 1.6". $400-600.
Center: Necklace with coral cameo with portrait of woman set in beaded necklace and elaborate frame, ca. 1890s. Coral drop and coral beads set in gold frames on chain, 1.5" x 1.7". $2500-3000.
Top right: Shell cameo pendant of woman's portrait, ca. 1890s. Set in frame with seed pearls and heavy frame with beads. 1.38" x 1.3". $225-295.
The cameos in this photograph are *Courtesy of The Patrician Antiques*.

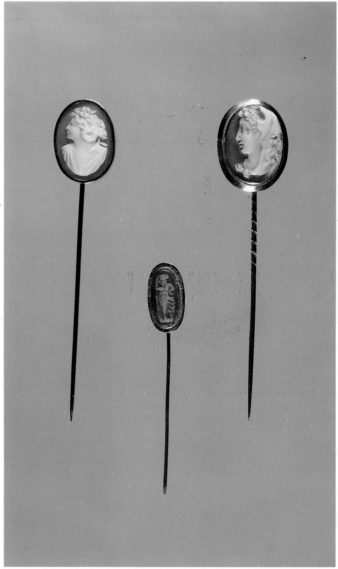

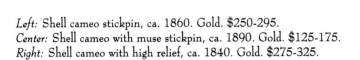

Left: Shell cameo stickpin, ca. 1860. Gold. $250-295.
Center: Shell cameo with muse stickpin, ca. 1890. Gold. $125-175.
Right: Shell cameo with high relief, ca. 1840. Gold. $275-325.

Top: Carnelian intaglio ring, ca. 1890. Ring is 10K gold, top measures .25" x .32". $900-1200.
Left center: Tiger eye cameo ring, ca. 1900. Ring is 14K gold, top .38" x .5". $800-900.
Center: Shell cameo ring, ca. 1900s. Ring is 14K gold, top .38" x .5". $700-800.
Right center: Shell cameo ring depicting full figure of woman, ca. 1900s. Ring is 14K gold, top .38" x .62". $900-1200.
Bottom: Shell cameo ring, ca. 1900s. Ring is 14K gold, top .75" x .88". $800-900.
The cameos in this photograph are *Courtesy of Shirley Falardeau.*

Left: Cameo habillé brooch of woman wearing diadem with five diamonds, ca. 1880s. Set in 18K gold Etruscan style beaded frame, 1.38" x 1.62". $1500-2000.
Top: Coral cameo locket/fob of woman with flowers in hair, ca. 1890s. Set in 14K gold frame with onyx stones, .75" x 1.12". $900-1200.
Bottom: Shell cameo brooch of woman with upswept hair, ca. 1920s. Set in decorated frame, 1.12" x 1.38". $700-900.
Right: Shell cameo pendant with full figure of woman holding flowers, ca. 1890s. Set in 18K gold frame, 1.38" x 1.75". $1200-1500.
The cameos in this photograph are *Courtesy of Frank and Dorothy Everts.*

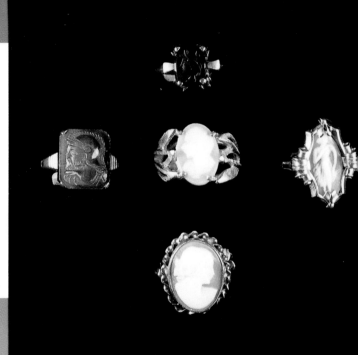

Top left: Shell cameo brooch of woman's portrait, ca. 1890s. Set in etched frame, .6" x .75". $250-425.
Top right: Shell cameo pendant of portrait of woman, ca. 1930s. Set in Etruscan style beaded frame, .62" x .8". $300-400.
Left: Shell cameo locket/pendant depicting mythological motif of the Three Muses, ca. 1940s. Set in twisted gold frame, 1" x 1.2". $400-500.
Lower center: Shell Florenza clip-on earrings with portrait of woman, ca. 1940s. Angular frames, .75" x .88". $150-175.
Right: Coral cameo pendant in high relief depicting woman adorned with flowers and wearing necklace, frame is pinchbeck, measures 1.12" x 1.25", ca. 1850s. $1500-2000.
The cameos in this photograph are *Courtesy of Bobby and Mary Fyffe.*

Top left: Shell screw-on earrings of woman with flower in hair, ca. 1920s. Twisted wire frames are sterling silver, .62" x .88". $125-175.

Top right: Stud shell cameo earrings with portrait of woman, ca. 1930s. Set in elaborate frames with flowers, .62" x .75". $150-225.

Center top: Cuff links with shell cameos of woman with flowers in hair and shoulder, ca. early 1900s. Set in twisted wire frames, .62" x .75". $225-300.

Left center: Shell cameo ring of woman with flower in hair, ca. 1890. Crosby 10K gold, .8" x .7". $400-500.

Center: Stone cameo ring of figure, ca. 1880s. 10K gold, .4" x .62". $450-600.

Right center: Shell cameo ring of woman, ca. 1890s. .7" x .88". $250-275.

Bottom left: Shell cameo ring with portrait, ca. 1920s. Sterling silver, .6" x .62". $200-300.

Bottom center: Shell cameo ring of woman, ca. 1930s. Silver metal with rhinestones, .75" x .9". $175-200.

Bottom right: Shell cameo ring of woman with flower on head, ca. 1920s. 10K gold, .62" x .8". $350-425.

The cameos in this photograph are *Courtesy of The Patrician Antiques*.

Top: Shell cameo portrait of Classical woman, ca. early 1900s. No frame, .5" x .7". $200-300.

Center left: Stone cameo pendant with portrait depicting woman in profile, ca. 1920s. Set in etched frame, .6" x .7". $250-350.

Center: Glass cameo brooch of woman with flowers in hair, ca. 1930s. Set in ornate frame, .7" x .88". $85-95.

Center right: Shell cameo pendant of woman with curls on top of head, ca. 1920s. Set in Etruscan style beaded frame, .7" x .88". $300-500.

Center left: Rebecca at the Well shell cameo pendant, ca. 1890s. Set in frame of fine twisted wire, .75" x .88". $250-350.

Center: Rebecca at the Well shell cameo brooch, ca. 1890s. Set in gold frame, .6" x .7". $275-425.

Center right: Rebecca at the Well shell cameo brooch with c clasp, ca. 1890s. Set in twisted ribbon frame, .75" x .88". $700-900.

Bottom left: Shell cameo pendant of woman in profile, ca. early 1900s. Set in frame with seed pearls, .75" x 1". $275-425.

Bottom center: Stone cameo pendant depicting woman in profile, ca. 1890s. Set in twisted wire frame, .62" x .88". $250-295.

Bottom right: Shell cameo pendant of woman with flower in hair, ca. 1920s. Set in frame with gold leaves, .75" x .9". $200-400.

The cameos in this photograph are *Courtesy of The Patrician Antiques*.

Chapter Five
Glass

Top: Earrings with recessed glass cameos depicting woman's portrait, ca. 1890s. Set in unusual frames with beading, measure 1.12" x 1.25". $195-250.

Bottom: Cameo habillé necklace with small diamond, ca. 1973. Frame is 14K gold, 24" chain, 1.62" in diameter. $400-500.

The cameos in this photograph are *Courtesy of Melissa A. Elrod.*

Top left: Coro earrings, ca. 1950s. Plastic cameos in beaded frame with rhinestones, .7" x .88". $175-195.

Top right: White plastic cameo clip-on earrings with portrait on dark background, ca. 1960s. Pearled frames, .75" in diameter. $75-95.

Bottom left and Bottom right: Glass cameo earrings, ca. 1910. Set in ornate frames decorated with flowers, .9" x 1.12". $195-225.

Center: Glass cameo brooch of woman in profile, ca. 1950s. Sparkling glass stones surround cameo and edge of brooch, 2.25" in diameter. $175-195.

The cameos in this photograph are *Courtesy of The Patrician Antiques.*

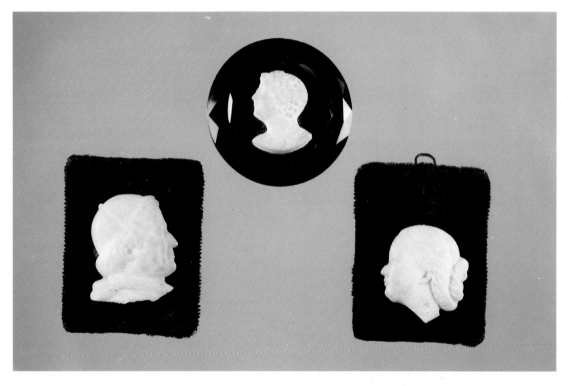

Bottom left: Glass cameo portrait of religious figure, ca. 1850s. Damaged cameo set on velvet, 1.5" x 1.8". $150-175.

Top center: Glass cameo portrait of German woman with flowers in hair, ca. 1890s. Cameo 1.5" in diameter. $95-125.

Bottom right: Glass cameo portrait pendant of woman, ca. 1850s. Damage to bottom of cameo, set on velvet, 1.75" x 1.88". $125-175.

The cameos in this photograph are *Courtesy of The Patrician Antiques.*

Top left: Glass cameo brooch of woman with flowers in hair, ca. 1890. Twisted wire frame and c clasp, 1.25" x 1.5". $225-250.
Center: Vermeil bracelet with five mother-of-pearl cameos depicting portrait of woman, ca. 1920s. Each cameo measures .62" in diameter. $425-495.

Right: Pink glass cameo brooch with portrait of woman, ca. 1915. Signed West Germany, brooch has c clasp, 1.62" x 1.88". $195-225.
The cameos in this photograph are *Courtesy of Melissa A. Elrod.*

Left: Glass cameo brooch depicting woman wearing head ornament, ca. 1860. Gold frame, 1.12" x 1.38". $275-295.
Center: Glass cameo brooch of woman with flower in hair, ca. 1890. Gold frame 1.3" x 1.6". $250-275.

Right: Glass cameo brooch depicting woman with flowers and leaves in hair, ca. 1890. Gold frame 1.1" x 1.38". $225-275.
The cameos in this photograph are *Courtesy of Kathleen Cunningham.*

Top: Celluloid cameo brooch, 1910. Gold metal frame with Etruscan style beading, 1.50" x 1.88". $95-150.
Bottom left: Clear glass molded cameo brooch/pendant on green glass background, ca. 1950. Twisted gold metal frame, 1.5" x 1.88". $75-95.
Bottom right: Glass over porcelain cameo pendant with foil back, ca. 1930. Twisted gold metal frame, 1.5" x 2". $65-75.

Top: Celluloid cameo pendant of portrait against fabric background, ca. 1950s. Frame of beaded pearls and glass stones, 1.25" x 1.5". $75-95.
Center: West German onyx cameo clip-on earrings, ca. 1950s. Set in beaded pearl frames, .88" x 1". $85-100.
Bottom: West German onyx brooch of woman in profile, ca. 1950s. Set in frame of beaded pearls and twisted wire, 1.62" x 2". $85-125.
The cameos in this photograph are *Courtesy of Margie M. Sparks*.

Left: Glass cameo brooch/pendant with profile of woman, ca. 1890. Gold frame, 1.25" x 1.5". $150-225.
Right: Glass cameo brooch/pendant depicting woman with elaborate hairstyle adorned with flowers, ca. 1890. Gold frame with some damage, 1.5" x 2". $95-125.
The cameos in this photograph are *Courtesy of Kathleen Cunningham.*

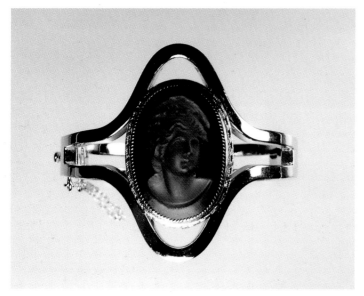

Cameo glass bracelet depicting woman's portrait in relief, ca. 1960s. Color of cameo is deep lavender, set in silver beaded and etched frame with outer frame of sloping shape. *Courtesy of Valerie Owen.* $275-295.

Assorted loose intaglio stones, 1900s. Range in price from $35-100.

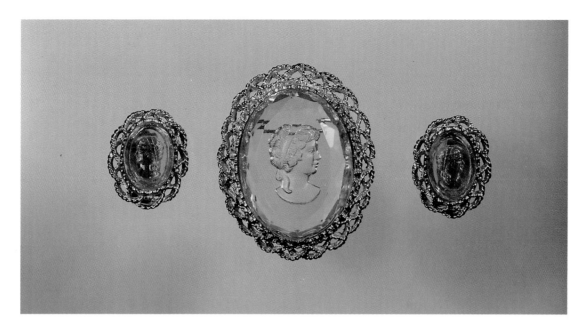

Pink glass cameo set of earrings and brooch, ca. 1970s. Set in gold metal frames, earrings .75" x 1.12", brooch 1.75" x 2.25". *Courtesy of Lorene Goetsch.* $95-150.

Left: Glass intaglio incised from back depicting woman in profile, ca. 1960s. Set in ornate frame with three tassels, 1.38" x 1.88", tassels 1.5". $45-55.
Right: Celluloid cameo stick pin with woman in profile, ca. 1915. Frame with colored stones, 1" x 1.25". $55-65.
The cameos in this photograph are *Courtesy of Lorene Goetsch.*

Whiting Davis set of clear glass, ca. 1960s. Cameo clip-on earrings .88" x 1.12", cameo pendant 1.75" x 2.12". Set in decorative silver mesh metal frames. *Courtesy of Lorene Goetsch.* $95-150.

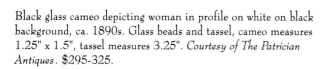

Top: Glass cameo brooch/pendant, ca. 1950s. Gold frame, 1.5" x 1.75", and chain is 10.5". $65-95.
Bottom left: Glass cameo pendant, ca. 1960s. Silver frame, 1.5" x 2" and chain, 12.25". $75-105.
Bottom right: Plastic pendant, ca. 1970s. Silver frame, 1.5" x 1.75", and chain, 9". $55-75.
The cameos in this photograph are *Courtesy of Lorene Goetsch*.

Black glass cameo depicting woman in profile on white on black background, ca. 1890s. Glass beads and tassel, cameo measures 1.25" x 1.5", tassel measures 3.25". *Courtesy of The Patrician Antiques*. $295-325.

Left: Glass intaglio brooch/pendant of portrait, ca. 1970s. Set in frame with glass stones, 1.75" x 2.12". $95-125.
Right: Enclosed intaglio brooch against turquoise background, ca. 1950s. Set in gold colored beaded frame, 1.62" x 2". *Courtesy of Margie M. Sparks.* $75-95.

Glass brooch/pendant, ca. 1960s. Four stones decorate frame, 1.75" x 2.25". *Courtesy of DeLorias Milam.* $95-125.

Left: Glass intaglio depicting mythological motif of Eros (Cupid) with bow and Artemis (Diana) with spear, ca. 1970s. Set in frame with leaves, 2" in diameter. $195-225.
Center: Glass cameo pendant depicting Classical figure, ca. 1960s. Set in gold wire frame, .88" x 1.12". $95-125.
Right: Glass cameo pendant depicting portrait of woman, ca. 1960s. 1.5" x 1.88". $125-175.
The cameos in this photograph are *Courtesy of The Patrician Antiques.*

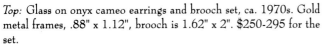

Top left: Glass cameo pendant of woman with flower on shoulder, ca. 1980s. Set in frame with twisted metal, 1.25" x 1.75". $85-95.
Bottom left: Glass intaglio pendant of woman in profile, ca. 1970s. Set in frame with glass stones, .88" in diameter. $95-125.
Right: Glass intaglio locket/pendant with woman's portrait and tassel, ca. 1970s. Frame with twisted wire and beads, 1.5" x 2". $125-150.
The cameos in this photograph are *Courtesy of The Patrician Antiques.*

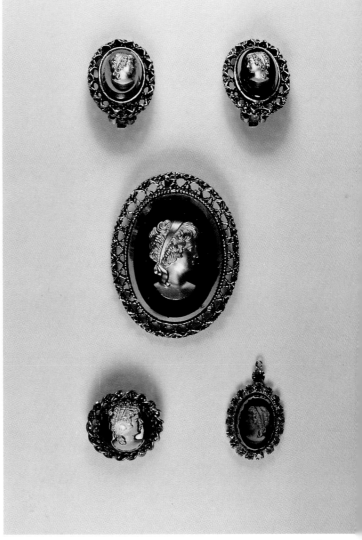

Top: Glass on onyx cameo earrings and brooch set, ca. 1970s. Gold metal frames, .88" x 1.12", brooch is 1.62" x 2". $250-295 for the set.
Bottom left: Signed Western Germany glass intaglio brooch, ca. 1920s. Twisted gold frame, 1" in diameter. $125-145.
Bottom right: Glass intaglio pendant, ca. 1960s. Silver frame with rhinestones, .75" x 1". $65-85.

Charcoal gray onyx cameo pendant, ca. 1970s. Frame filigree gold tone with pearls and black onyx stones, 1.25" x 1.75". *Courtesy of Nell Palmer Orr*. $265-295.

Left: Glass cameo necklace by Trafari depicting floral motif with butterfly, ca. 1980s. Silver frame, 1.12" x 1.5", and 20" chain. $95-125.
Top: Glass cameo brooch of two Classical warrior figures, ca. 1940s. Sterling back and frame, 1" diameter. $150-175.
Bottom: Plastic cameo earrings of woman in profile, ca. 1940s. $75-95.
The cameos in this photograph are *Courtesy of Shirley Falardeau*.

White molded glass cameo brooch depicting mythological motif of Psyche with butterfly wings in hair and on shoulder, ca. 1910. Frame of gold with brass tone, 2.75" x 2". $195-225.

Whiting Davis glass cameo set, ca. 1960s. Cameos set in twisted metal frames with beads, earrings 1" x 1.12", pendant 1.75" x 2.5". *Courtesy of Lorene Goetsch.* $175-195.

Top: Crystal intaglio set, ca. 1970s. Earrings .25" x .75", pendant .75" x 1". $55-85.
Bottom: Whiting Davis earrings, ca. 1960s. Set in gold mesh metal frames, .88" x 1.25". $65-85.
The cameos in this photograph are *Courtesy of Lorene Goetsch.*

Bakelite cameo on lavaliere, ca. of cameo 1930s. Gold metal frame, 1" x 1.12". *Courtesy of Shirley Falardeau.* $145-225.

Top: Crystal intaglio, ca. 1960s. Silver metal, .88" in diameter. $125-150.
Bottom: Glass intaglio earrings, ca 1970s. Set in frames of pewter, 1" x .88". $75-95.
The cameos in this photograph are *Courtesy of Shirley Falardeau.*

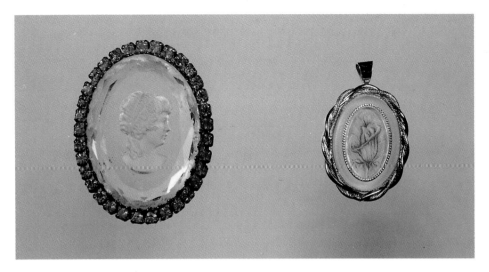

Left: Glass intaglio brooch/pendant of woman in profile, ca. 1900s. Rhinestones are set in gold frame, 1.5" x 2". $125-150.
Right: Quartz intaglio pendant depicting floral motif with flower incised, ca. 1900s. Gold frame has Etruscan style granulation and twisted rope effect, .88" x 1.38", $195-225.
The intaglios in this photograph are *Courtesy of Antiques By Daisy.*

Top: Glass intaglio pendant with profile of woman, ca. 1970. Gold metal frame with tassel, 1.25" x 1.5". $75-85.
Bottom left: Glass intaglio pendant with flowers, ca. 1970. Gold metal frame, 1.25" x 1.5". $65-75.
Bottom right: Glass intaglio pendant with figure of woman and dog signed Avon, ca. 1970. Silver metal frame, 1.25" x 1.5". $85-95.
The intaglios in this photograph are *Courtesy of Mary Moon, Red Wagon Antiques.*

Top left: Glass molded intaglio brooch with woman's portrait, ca. 1980s. Silver metal frame 1.38" x 1.5". $55-75.
Top right: Glass molded intaglio brooch of woman in profile, ca. 1980s. Silver metal mesh frame, 1.12" x 1.38". $45-55.
Center: Glass molded intaglio with woman's portrait, ca. 1970s. Gold metal frame, 1.75" x 2". $30-45.
Bottom left: Celluloid cameo brooch of woman with flowers in hair, ca. 1930. Silver die stamped frame, 1.38" x 1.75". $85-95.
Bottom right: Mother-of-pearl cameo brooch depicting woman with short hairstyle wearing flower in hair, ca. 1930. Twisted effect die stamped brass frame, 1.25" x 1.75". $100-150.

Topaz intaglio pendant, ca. 1930s. Gold frame with beading, 1.62"
x 2". *Courtesy of Lenora Alice Knighton.* $225-275.

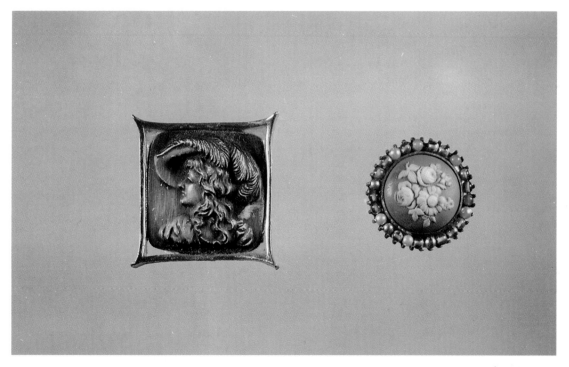

Left: Hobe blue cameo depicting man wearing plumed hat, ca.
1960s. Set in square frame, 1.62" square. $75-95.
Right: Jaspar ware cameo depicting floral motif in relief, ca. 1950s.
Set in frame with stones and pearls, measures 1.2" in diameter. $95-
125.
The cameos in this photograph are *Courtesy of The Patrician
Antiques.*

Amber glass intaglio necklace, ca. 1980s. Gold frame, 1.5" x 2" and chain, 24". *Courtesy of Great Finds & Designs, Inc. of Texarkana.* $65-75.

Amber glass cameo pendant of woman in profile, ca. 1930s. Gold metal frame with beading, 1.62" x 2" and newer chain, 24" long. *Courtesy of Sarah Newton.* $75-95.

Clear glass intaglio incised from back of piece, ca. 1980s. Gold metal frame with white enameling and twisted effect, 2" in diameter. *Courtesy of Nana Dodds.* $75-85.

Whiting Davis glass cameo pendant with tassel, ca. 1960s. Set in gold frame, cameo measures 1.35" x 1.5", tassel measures 1.38". *Courtesy of George and Dotty Stringfield.* $85-95.

Left: Whiting Davis glass brooch/pendant with tassel of woman in profile with flower on shoulder, ca. 1960s. Set in silver frame, 1.12" x 1.25". $85-95.
Right: Glass cameo pendant of deep lavender (color in photograph is not true) depicting woman's portrait in relief, ca. 1960s. Set in silver beaded and etched frame with outer frame of sloping shape. $275-295.
The cameos in this photograph are *Courtesy of Valerie Owen.*

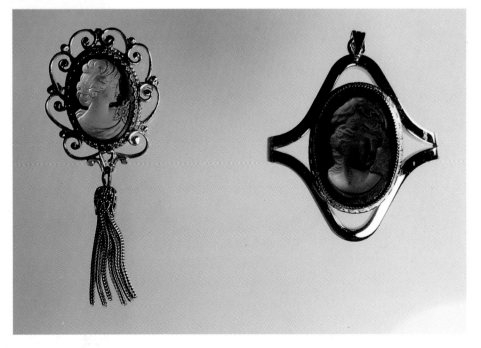

West Germany glass cameo pendant and earring set, ca. 1960s. Gold metal frames with seed pearls, pendant is 2" x 2.5" and earrings are 1" x 1.25". *Courtesy of Lorene Goetsch.* $175-195.

Top: Glass cameo pendant, ca. 1930s. Set in silver metal frame, .75" x 1". $55-65.
Center: Plastic cameo clip-on earrings, ca. 1960s. Frames are gold with dangles, .75" in diameter. $75-85.
Bottom left: Plastic cameo pendant, ca. 1940s. Set in gold metal frame with beading, 1.25" x 1.75" and chain 12". $65-85.
Bottom right: Cameo plastic on glass pendant, ca. 1960s. Set in gold frame, 1.75" x 2" and chain, 12". $65-85.
The cameos in this photograph are *Courtesy of Lorene Goetsch.*

Whiting Davis high relief frosted quartz cameo set with pendant and clip-on earrings, ca. 1960s. Pendant 1.5" x 2" and earrings .75" x 1" set in silver metal frames. *Courtesy of Lorene Goetsch.* $175-195.

Top left: Glass intaglio earrings with woman's portrait, ca. 1930s. Set in gold frames, .62" x .88". $150-175.
Top right: Glass intaglio earrings of woman, ca. 1930s. Set in Sterling silver frames, .6" x .5". $125-150.
Bottom left: Glass intaglio pendant of woman in profile, ca. 1940s. Set in silver frame, 1.5" x 2.12". $125-150.
Bottom center: Cameos of reddish stone with beading, ca. early

1900s. Set in frames with turquoise stones, measure .62" x 1.25". $195-225.
Bottom right: Glass intaglio brooch of woman, ca. 1960s. Some damage to bottom center of brooch, 1.62" x 2.12". $85-95.
The cameos in this photograph are *Courtesy of The Patrician Antiques*.

Left: Cameo of Czechoslovakian glass brooch depicting woman, ca. 1890s. Set in gold frame with safety clasp, 1.25" x 1.5". $125-150.
Center top: Bar pin with glass cameo of woman set in beaded frame, ca. 1920s. Pin has decorative beads at either end, pin has safety clasp, 1.25" long. $125-150.
Center bottom: Locket/necklace with onyx intaglio depicting soldier, ca. 1920s. Set in heavy beaded frame with carnelian stone on back, .65" x .88". $500-700.
Right: Cameo pendant of jet depicting soldier, ca. early 1900s. Set in gold tone frame, 1.75" x 1.88". $125-150.
The cameos in this photograph are *Courtesy of The Patrician Antiques*.

Left: Glass cameo brooch depicting woman with child and animal, ca. 1960s. Frame with twisted wire, 1.62" x 2". $85-95.
Right: Glass cameo pendant, portrait of woman, ca. 1960s. Frame with twisted wire, 1.5" x 2". $65-85.
The cameos in this photograph are *Courtesy of The Patrician Antiques*.

View of carnelian stone at the back of onyx locket/necklace, set in heavy beaded frame, measures .65" x .88", ca. 1920s. *Courtesy of The Patrician Antiques.* $500-700.

Chapter Six
Various Materials

Bone cameo brooch with flower, ca. 1920. Carved frame with clear stones, some missing, 1.25" x 1.75". *Courtesy of Louise Martin*. $85-95.

Left: Jet cameo brooch portrait of woman, measures 2.25" x 2.25", ca. early 1890s. $175-195.
Right: Czechoslovakia black glass circular cameo brooch with c clasp depicting woman, measures 1.62" in diameter, ca. 1880. $95-125. The cameos in this photograph are *Courtesy of The Patrician Antiques*.

Top: Jet cameo portrait with c clasp with mythological motif of Medusa, ca. 1840. Rectangular frame, 1.5" x 1.75". $295-325.
Bottom left: Celluloid portrait of a woman, ca. 1920s. 1.25" x 1.62". $125-150.
Bottom right: Cameo locket/pendant portrait made of jet in high relief, ca. 1890s. Decorated gold frame, 1.5" x 1.88". $300-400. The cameos in this photograph are *Courtesy of Melissa A. Elrod.*

Top left: Stone cameo brooch of woman's portrait, ca. 1840-60. Gold beaded frame, 1.25" x 1.5". $350-425.
Top right: Coral cameo brooch depicting mythological motif of Bacchante maiden, follower of Dionysus (Bacchus), god of wine and fertility, with grapes and grape leaves in hair, ca. 1890. Frame in 10K gold, 1.25" x 1.62". Some damage. $325-350.
Center: Onyx cameo brooch of woman with flowers in hair, ca. 1840-60. Twisted gold frame, 1.5" x 2". $425-450.
Bottom left: Glass cameo brooch of woman adorned with flowers, ca. 1870. Gold frame, 1.38" x 1.63". $125-195.
Bottom right: Stone cameo brooch/pendant of woman in profile, ca. 1915. Gold frame, 1.12" x 1.5". $500-600.

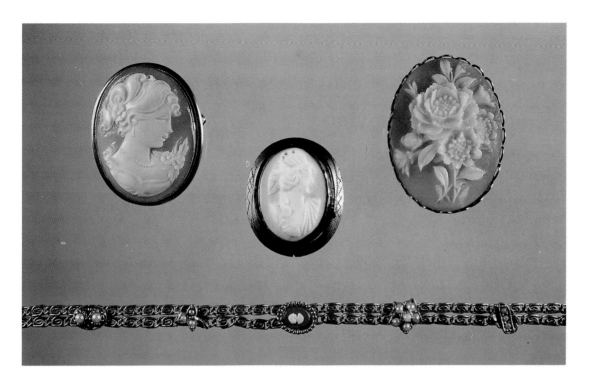

Left: Shell cameo brooch/pendant of woman adorned with flowers in hair and on shoulders, ca. 1920s. Frame is sterling silver 800, measures 1.25" x 1.5". $395-425.

Center: Shell cameo brooch depicting mythological motif of Psyche with butterfly wing, ca. early 1900s. Set in etched frame, measures 1.12" x 1.25". $425-450.

Right: Plastic cameo depicting floral motif, ca. 1960s. Twisted wire frame, 1.25" x 1.7". $65-95.

Bottom: Bracelet with beaded pearls, stones, and cameo portrait of woman, ca. 1950s. Set in beaded frame, cameo measures .38" x .4". *Courtesy of Patricia Farren.* $65-85.

Unless otherwise noted, the cameos in this photograph are *Courtesy of Margie M. Sparks.*

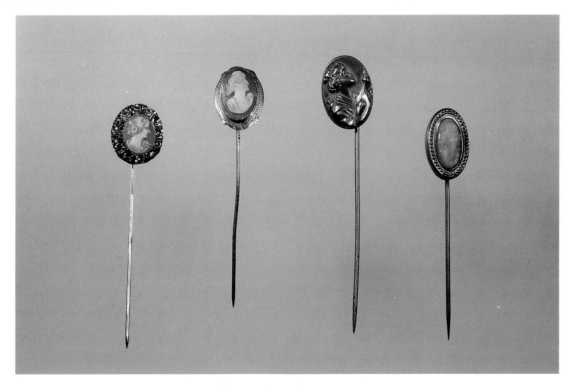

Left: Shell cameo stickpin of woman wearing flowers in hair and on shoulder, ca. 1930s. Gold. $195-235.

Center left: Shell cameo stickpin depicting mythological motif of Artemis (Diana), goddess of the hunt, with crescent moon on head, ca. 1860. Gold. $295-325.

Center right: Gold relief stickpin of woman playing lute, ca. 1910. $175-195.

Right: Stone cameo stickpin of woman's portrait in relief, ca. 1915. Gold frame has beading. $225-245.

The cameos in this photograph are *Courtesy of Antiques By Daisy.*

Top: Shell cameo earrings, ca. 1930s. Set in twisted wire frames, with steel dangles. $150-175.
Center: Carved ivory cameo ring in relief of Oriental figure, ca. 1880s. Set in gold. *Courtesy of Jackie McDonald.* $525-575.
Bottom: Book chain with stone cameo of woman in profile, ca. 1880s. Set in ornate frame with pearl drop. *Courtesy of Jackie McDonald.* $825-895.

Left: Stone brooch depicting mythological motif of Psyche with butterfly wing, ca. 1880s. Colorful beading, set in unusual frame, 1.88" x 2.3". $525-595.
Right: Shell brooch with portrait of woman with flower in hair and on garment, ca. 1915. Frame with filigree, 1/120 12K GF, 1.38" x 1.62". $695-725.
The cameo brooches in this photograph are *Courtesy of Donna Hanner.*

Left: White on orange glass cameo depicting mythological motif of Psyche with butterfly wings in hair, ca. 1890s. Oval, 1.38" x 1.75". $125-145.
Center: Shell cameo depicting mythological motif of Bacchante maiden, follower of Dionysus (Bacchus), god of wine and fertility, with grapes and grape leaves in hair, ca. 1890s. Set in decorated frame, 1.38" x 1.75". $275-295.
Right: Glass cameo of woman adorned with flowers, ca. 1890s. Set in rectangular frame with twisted wire effect, some damage to cameo, 1.25" x 1.62". $125-150.
The cameos in this photograph are *Courtesy of Antiques by Daisy.*

Cameo in gold relief of Classical figure, ca. 1860. Set against mother-of-pearl background. *Courtesy of Melissa A. Elrod.* $295-325.

Top left: Tiger eye intaglio ring depicting soldier, ca. 1860. Ring 14K gold, .62" square on top. *Courtesy of Margie Sparks.* $800-900.

Top right: Shell cameo ring of woman in profile, ca. 1900. Gold ring, .5" on top. $150-325.

Center: Shell cameo brooch, ca. 1860. Rolled gold frame, 1.12" x 1.25". *Courtesy of Margie Sparks.* $225-375.

Bottom left: Tiger eye cameo ring with two profiles, ca. 1840-60. Ring 14K gold, .62" square on top. $700-800.

Bottom right: Plastic cameo ring, ca. 1970. $55-85.

Left: Coral cameo brooch, ca. 1950s. Silver brooch, 3" x 1.88", and cameo, .25" x .5". $65-85.

Right: Shell cameo brooch depicting mythological motif of Artemis (Diana), goddess of the hunt, with crescent moon in hair, ca. 1930s. Gold frame with twisted ribbon effect, bow attached to frame, 1" x 1.38". $325-375.

The cameos in this photograph are *Courtesy of Shirley Falardeau.*

Top: Milk glass cameo brooch, ca. 1840. Gold frame, 1" in diameter. $150-175.
Bottom: Agate cameo dress clip of young girl, ca. 1930s. Frame RGP, 1.5" x 1.75". $350-395.
The cameos in this photograph are *Courtesy of Shirley Falardeau.*

Top left: Loose glass cameo of Classical figure, ca. 1930s. Oval cameo, .3" x .75". $35-45.
Top center: Red stone square intaglio cuff link of woman, ca. 1930s. .62". $95-150.
Top right: Amber glass cameo, ca. 1930s. .5" x .6". $25-35.
Left: White on black celluloid brooch of woman, ca. 1940s. .88" x 1.12". $45-55.
Center left: White stone of Roman woman, ca. 1920s, .38" x .5". $35-45.
Center right: Onyx cameo of Roman figure, ca. 1920s, .33" x .4". $45-55.
Right: Celluloid cameo of woman's portrait, ca. 1940s, .35" x .92". $30-40.
The cameos and intaglios in this photograph are *Courtesy of Sandy Burnett.*

Top: Obsidian cameo brooch of woman wearing head ornament, ca. 1840-60. Silver back and prongs signed DB, 1.12" in diameter. $200-300.
Bottom: Plastic cameo brooch habillé of woman wearing necklace, ca. 1930s. Silver frame, 1.12" x 1.62". $85-95.
The cameos in this photograph are *Courtesy of Shirley Falardeau.*

144

Top: Gold metal relief cameo depicting mythological motif of Dionysus (Bacchus), god of wine and fertility, ca. 1860. Measures 1.5" x 2". $400-500.

Bottom left: Milk glass cameo brooch/pendant of woman in profile, ca. 1915. Frame is sterling silver, 1.5" x 2". $225-250.

Bottom right: Jet cameo brooch with profile of woman, ca. 1890. Gold frame with beading, 1.61" x 2". $400-500.

The cameos in this photograph are *Courtesy of Sue Rainey Pruitt*.

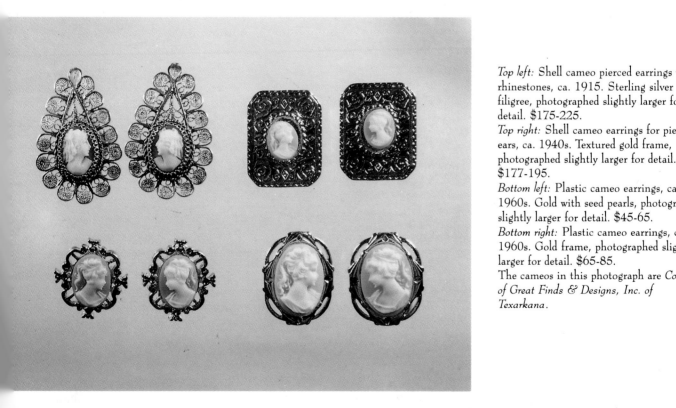

Top left: Shell cameo pierced earrings with rhinestones, ca. 1915. Sterling silver filigree, photographed slightly larger for detail. $175-225.

Top right: Shell cameo earrings for pierced ears, ca. 1940s. Textured gold frame, photographed slightly larger for detail. $177-195.

Bottom left: Plastic cameo earrings, ca. 1960s. Gold with seed pearls, photographed slightly larger for detail. $45-65.

Bottom right: Plastic cameo earrings, ca. 1960s. Gold frame, photographed slightly larger for detail. $65-85.

The cameos in this photograph are *Courtesy of Great Finds & Designs, Inc. of Texarkana*.

Top: Clip-on earrings with plastic cameos, ca. 1940s. Set in frames with beaded and twisted wire frames, .88" x 1.12". $75-85.
Center left: Shell cameo brooch of woman wearing pearls, ca. 1915. Set in detailed gold frame, 1.12" x 1.3". $395-425.
Center right: Plastic cameo brooch of woman's portrait, ca. 1960s. Missing pin, .75" x 1". $35-45.
Bottom: Shell cameo pendant necklace with portrait of woman, ca. 1920s. Cameo in filigree frame, .6" x .8". $250-350.
The cameos in this photograph are *Courtesy of The Patrician Antiques.*

Top left: Gold metal relief star brooch with face of a Gibson Girl and five stones at points, ca. 1900. Gold metal, 1" in diameter. $250-350.
Top right: Plastic cameo brooch of woman in profile on jet background, ca. 1930s. Shell frame, 1.75" in diameter. $85-95.
Center left: Jet cameo brooch with profile of woman, ca. 1840. Gold metal frame, 1.75" in diameter. $225-250.
Center right: Onyx and gold cameo cuff links, ca. 1890. Gold frame, .56" x .75". $195-225.
Bottom left: Jet cameo brooch, ca. 1930. Rectangular gold metal frame, 1.88" x 2.38". $275-295.
Bottom right: Moonstone cameo brooch, ca. 1840. Gold frame, .69" x .88". $175-195.

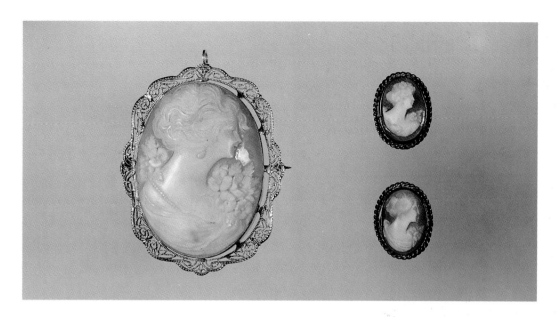

Left: Shell cameo/brooch pendant depicting woman with flowers, ca. early 1900s. Silver filigree frame, 1.75" x 2.25". $700-800.
Right: Stone cameo clip-on earrings with different profiles of women, ca. 1900. Twisted gold frame, .62" x .88". $495-525.
The cameos in this photograph are *Courtesy of Zelle H. Moore.*

Left: Shell pendant of woman in profile, ca. 1890. Twisted wire frame with ribbon effect, 1" x 1.25". $400-500.
Top center: Plastic heart shaped cameo earrings with portrait of woman, ca. 1940s. White with blue background, .5" x .5". $45-55.
Top right: Shell pendant of woman's portrait, ca. 1920s. Set in gold frame, .6" x 1.22". $225-295.
Center bottom: Shell brooch/pendant of woman in profile, ca. 1930. Set in frame with twisted wire, .62" x 1.25". $395-425.
Bottom right: Shell brooch/pendant depicting woman with flowers in hair and on shoulder, ca. 1915. Set in diagonally shaped filigree frame, 1.3" x 1.62". $500-600.
The cameos in this photograph are *Courtesy of Roland Hill.*

Left: Watch with glass cameos depicting generalized women's portraits, ca. 1980. $55-75.
Center: Plastic cameo on key ring, ca. 1890s. Silver metal, 1" in diameter. $45-55.
Right: Onyx cameo necklace, ca. 1930s. No frame, .88" x 1.12". $125-145.
The cameos in this photograph are *Courtesy of Mary Sax.*

Top: Gold relief earrings, ca. 1920s. Gold is 14K, .62" x .75. *Courtesy of Lynne Byrd Spivey.* $400-500.
Center: Shell brooch depicting mythological motif of Demeter (Ceres) with sheath of wheat, ca. 1890. Set in decorated octagonal frame, 1.25' x 1.5". $500-600.
Bottom left: Shell brooch/pendant with portrait of woman, ca. 1915. Signed Italy 925, .75" x .9". $395-425.
Bottom right: Shell cameo necklace, ca. 1920. Set in heart shaped frame, .88" x .88". $200-300.
Unless otherwise noted, the cameos in this photograph are *Courtesy of Sue Rainey Pruitt.*

Top: Shell cameo earrings with different profiles, ca. 1940s. Sterling frame, 1" x 1.25". $195-225.
Center: Glass cameo brooch depicting woman with flowers in hair, ca. 1915. Gold frame, 1.12" x 1.38". $175-195.
Bottom: Shell cameo on bracelet, ca. 1930. Gold mesh bracelet with cameo measuring .66" x .75". $125-150.
The cameos in this photograph are *Courtesy of Mary Sax*.

Left: Shell cameo bar pin, ca. 1840-60. Gold plated, 1.75" x .75". $400-500.
Center: Shell cameo pendant, ca. 1915. Sterling silver frame, .88" x 1". $200-300.
Right: Angel skin coral cameo brooch, ca. 1890. 14K gold, 2" x 1.25". $250-350.
The cameos in this photograph are *Courtesy of Shirley Falardeau*.

Top left: Shell cameo brooch, ca. 1890. Frame gold, .75" x 1". $300-400.

Top right: Stone cameo stickpin depicting helmeted figure, ca. 1860. Gold, .5" x .75", pin 1.5" long. $250-275.

Center: Loose shell cameo depicting Hermes (Mercury), messenger for the gods with winged hat, ca. 1890. 1.25" x 1.5". $275-295.

Bottom left: Shell cameo brooch depicting mythological motif of Psyche with butterfly wing in hair, ca. 1860. Gold octagonal frame, 1.25" x 1". $400-500.

Bottom right: Onyx cameo locket/pendant with two faces in black and white depicting night and day, ca. 1890. Gold, .75" x 1". $300-400.

The cameos in this photograph are *Courtesy of Jackie McDonald.*

Top left: Agate cameo brooch of woman with flower on shoulder, ca. 1900. Set in new 14K gold frame, 1.25" x 1.62". $500-600.

Top right: Shell cameo brooch of woman wearing head ornament, ca. 1840. Gold frame 1.12" x 1.5". $350-400.

Center: Shell cameo bar pin, ca. 1860. RGP frame, 2.38" x .75". $500-600.

Bottom left: Shell cameo brooch of woman with flower in hair, ca. early 1900s. Gold frame, 1.75" in diameter. $200-300.

Bottom right: Shell cameo brooch of woman in profile, ca. 1940. Gold frame with pearls, 1.75" x .88". $250-350.

Cameos in this photograph are *Courtesy of Shirley Falardeau.*

Top left: Shell cameo brooch with woman with flower on shoulder, ca. 1930s. Set in beaded octagonal frame, .7" x .9". $395-495.

Top center: Pink coral cameo brooch of woman adorned with flowers, ca. early 1900s. Set in twisted wire frame, .9" x 1.2". $300-400.

Top right and Bottom right: Plastic cameo earrings depicting woman looking at flower on her shoulder, ca. 1950s. Set in dark plastic frames, .88" x 1.2". $65-75.

Bottom left: Shell cameo ring depicting woman in profile, ca. 1880s. 10K gold, .88" x 1.2". $500-600.

Bottom center: Coral cameo pendant of woman's portrait, ca. 1890s. With four jade stones, 1" x 1.25". $400-500.

The cameos in this photograph are *Courtesy of The Patrician Antiques.*

Left: Plastic cameo pendant of woman in profile, ca. 1950s. Set in twisted wire frame, .9" x 1.2". $85-125.

Center: Stick pin with glass cameo of woman's profile, ca. 1940s. Set in plated frame, cameo measures .5" x .62", pin length is 2.1". $150-250.

Right: Shell cameo pendant of woman, ca. 1920s. Set in filigree frame, .95" x 1.3". $300-400.

The cameos in this photograph are *Courtesy of Frank and Dorothy Everts.*

Left: Shell cameo brooch, ca. 1930s. Gold metal frame, 1.12" x 1.62". $300-400.

Center: Celluloid cameo brooch, ca. 1930s. Measures 1.12" in diameter. $95-125.

Right: Shell cameo brooch, ca. 1940s. Gold frame, 1.1" x 1.3". $200-300.

The cameos in this photograph are *Courtesy of Antiques By Daisy.*

Top: Heart shaped plastic cameo charm, ca. 1950s. Silver frame, .38" x .5". $45-55.

Left: Glass cameo pendant depicting Florence Nightingale, ca. 1880s. No frame, 1.2" x .88". $95-125.

Right: Glass cameo white on black pendant of woman in profile, ca. 1920s. Set in beaded gold frame, 1" x 1.12"..$85-125.

Bottom: Plastic white on black cameo earrings, ca. 1950s. No frames, .5" x .75". $55-65.

The cameos in this photograph are *Courtesy of George and Dotty Stringfield.*

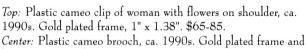

Top left: Shell cameo pendant, ca. 1915. Sterling silver frame, 1.38" x 1.75". $295-425.
Top right: Shell cameo pendant, ca. 1890. Gold metal entwined with seed pearls on frame, 1" x 1.12". $350-400.
Bottom: Sarah Coventry plastic cameo brooch/pendant, ca. 1970s. Gold metal frame, 1.5" x 2". $65-85.
The cameos in this photograph are *Courtesy of Great Finds & Designs, Inc. of Texarkana.*

Top: Plastic cameo clip of woman with flowers on shoulder, ca. 1990s. Gold plated frame, 1" x 1.38". $65-85.
Center: Plastic cameo brooch, ca. 1990s. Gold plated frame and bow, 1" x 1.25". $55-75.
Bottom: Plastic cameo necklace, ca. 1990s. Gold plated frame, 1.25" x 1.25", and chain, 16". $75-95.

Top: Glass cameo clip-on earrings, ca. 1970s. Frames enameled with white beads, .88" x 1". $65-85.
Top center: Plastic cameo brooch, ca. 1970s. Set in gold metal on black frame, 1.75" in diameter. $65-75.
Bottom: Plastic cameo bracelet, ca. 1970s. Cameos set in silver metal with rhinestones. $85-125.
The cameos in this photograph are *Courtesy of Lorene Goetsch.*

Top: Glass cameo brooch, ca. 1940s. Set in gold metal frame with beaded edge, 1" x 1.25". $50-60.
Bottom: White on black plastic earrings, ca. 1950s. Set in silver metal frames, 1" x 1.25". $55-65.
The cameos in this photograph are *Courtesy of Lorene Goetsch.*

Top left: Stone cameo brooch, ca. 1840s. Frame is 10K gold with Etruscan style beading around cameo, .88" x 1.25". $450-550.

Top right: Shell cameo brooch/pendant with profiles of Queen Elizabeth II and Prince Philip, ca. 1950s. Gold frame is 10K gold, .88" x 1.25". $400-500.

Center: Angel skin coral cameo pendant depicting mythological motif of Demeter (Ceres), goddess of the harvest, with sheath of wheat, ca. 1860. Gold frame with twisted effect, 1.38" x 1.75" $400-500.

Bottom left: Stone cameo brooch depicting mythological motif of Psyche with butterfly wing in hair, ca. 1915. Frame is 10K gold with seed pearls, 1.5" x 1.75". $400-500.

Bottom right: Angel skin coral cameo brooch/pendant depicting mythological motif of Demeter (Ceres), goddess of the harvest, with sheath of wheat in hair, ca. 1930s. Gold frame not original, 1.25" x 1.38". $250-350.

The cameos in this photograph are *Courtesy of Shirley Falardeau.*

Top left: Shell cameo stick pin, ca. 1860. Gold back and pin, .5" x .64". $225-295.

Top right: Shell cameo stick pin, ca. 1860. Gold frame and pin. $125-235.

Bottom left: Coral cameo habillé stick pin with diamond, depicts mythological motif of Bacchante maiden, follower of Dionysus (Bacchus), god of wine and fertility, with grapes and grape leaves in hair, ca. 1840. Gold backing and pin, .62" x .80". $275-325.

Bottom center: Stone cameo stick pin with profile of Queen Victoria, ca. 1880. Gold frame and pin, .5"x.75". $250-350.

Bottom right: Jet cameo stick pin with profile of warrior, ca. 1860. Gold frame and pin, .62" x .88". $125-235.

The cameos in this photograph are *Courtesy of Great Finds & Designs, Inc. of Texarkana.*

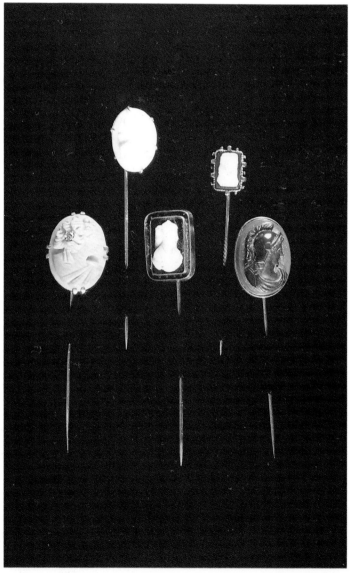

Top: Celluloid cameo earrings, ca. 1930s. Gold frames with 12 stones around each, 1" in diameter. $95-125.

Center left and right: Celluloid cameo earrings, ca. 1930s. Gold frames with stones, .63" x .88", $85-95.

Center: Onyx cameo ring, ca. 1890. Ring 1/20K R.G.P., .50" x .75". $300-400.

Center left: Celluloid cameo brooch, ca. 1910. Gold frame, 1" x 1.25". $85-125.

Center right: Onyx cameo pendent dangling from pin spelling Mother, ca. 1930. Gold pin, 1.75" wide and frame with rhinestones, 1" in diameter. $195-225.

Bottom left: Onyx cameo pendant dangling from bow pin, ca. 1930s. Gold bow, 1.25" x .75" and frame, .50" x .75". $175-250.

Bottom right: Onyx cameo bar pin, ca. 1870. Gold frame, .25" x .50"and pin, .88" long. $125-150.

Top: Molded glass cameo locket opening to back, depicts mythological motif of Psyche with butterfly wing in hair, ca. 1910. Frame gold with enameling, 1.38" x 1.75". $325-425.

Center: Hard stone cameo brooch, ca. 1916. Attached to frame of same era, 2" x 1.5". $125-300.

Bottom left: Tassie cameo brooch depicting mythological motif of Bacchante maiden, follower of Dionysus (Bacchus), god of wine and fertility, with grapes and grape leaves in hair, ca. 1840. Gold frame damaged,1.25" x 1.5". $400-450.

Bottom right: Small stone cameo pendant, 1950. Silver frame has blue stones, 1.5" x .62". $65-75.

Bottom right: Stone intaglio watch fob with head of warrior incised, ca. 1850. Metal wire circles the fob and is twisted to form a loop at top, .75" in diameter. $150-175.

Top: Shell cameo brooch with scene, ca. 1890. Gold metal frame with twisted wire around, 1" x 1.38". $300-350.
Center left: Shell cameo brooch with Three Muses, ca. 1890. Gold metal die-stamped frame, 1.5" x 1.75". $300-400.
Center right: Plastic molded cameo brooch of woman, ca. 1970. Gold metal frame, 1.5" x 1.75". $65-85.
Bottom: Glass molded cameo painted, ca. 1890. Twisted gold frame, 1.12" x 1.38". $85-105.

Top left and right: White on blue plastic earrings, ca. 1950. Silver frame, .75" x 1". $65-75.
Center top: Plastic pendant, ca. 1940s. White on blue with gold frame, bow with pearl, .88" x 1". $65-85.
Center: Plastic brooch signed Hattie Carnegie depicting mythological motif of Aphrodite (Venus) with Eros (Cupid), ca. 1970s. White on black with gold frame, 1.63" x 2". $95-125.
Bottom left: Plastic brooch, ca. 1980s. White on black with gold frame, .75" x 1". $45-65.
Bottom center: Plastic brooch/pendant signed Perri, ca. 1980s. White on blue background with gold metal frame, 1" x 1.38". $55-65.
Bottom right: Cobalt stone cameo for slide bracelet, ca. 1980. Gold twisted frame and fittings on back for slide, .63" x .75". $175-195.

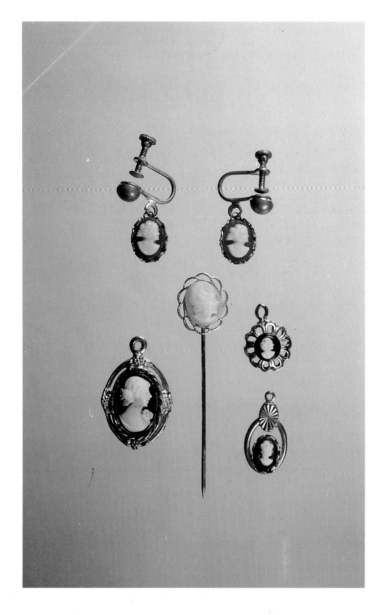

Top: Plastic cameo earrings, ca. 1930s. Gold frame, .38" x .5". $65-95.
Center: Shell Cameo stick pin, ca. 1915. Gold frame, .38" x .5". $95-125.
Center right: Plastic pendant, ca. 1930s. Gold frame, .62". $45-55.
Bottom left: Onyx cameo pendant, ca. 1930s. Gold frame, .75" x .88". $125-150.
Bottom right: Plastic cameo pendant, ca. 1930s. Gold frame, .5" x .75. $40-60.
The cameos in this photograph are *Courtesy of Shirley Falardeau.*

Top: Signed Made in Germany glass molded cameo set of earrings and brooch, ca. 1960s. Cameos set in gold metal with pearls and amber stones, earrings .88" x 1"and brooch 1.88" in diameter. $95-125 for set.
Center left: Faceted quartz intaglio pendant with profile of woman, ca. 1970s. Gold metal, 88" x 1.62". $175-195.
Center right: Stone cameo applied to brown stone, depicts mythological motif of Psyche with butterfly wing in hair, ca. 1930s. Gold frame with claw setting, 1.38" x 1.63". $155-175.
Bottom left: Amber colored glass intaglio earrings, ca. 1970s. Gold metal, .75" x .88". $75-95.
Bottom right: Topaz cameo fob depicting Roman warrior, ca. 1890. Cameo recessed in stone, 1.12" x 1". $250-275.

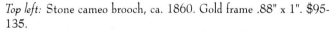

Top: Gutta-percha cameo brooch of muse with birds, ca. 1890. Silver frame, 1.5" x 1.88". $200-300.
Bottom: Coro cameo brooch/locket, ca. 1930s. Antique style decorative frame, 3" x 1". $150-200.
The cameos in this photograph are *Courtesy of Melissa A. Elrod.*

Top left: Stone cameo brooch, ca. 1860. Gold frame .88" x 1". $95-135.
Top center: Glass cameo pin, ca. 1940. Silver metal frame, .38" x .80" and bow, 1.5" wide. $65-95.
Top right: Stone cameo pendant is an early Gorham piece signed Martelé Sterling, ca. 1840. Sterling silver frame has stones surrounding the cameo, .75" x 1". $450-650.
Center: Shell cameo brooch/pendant in medium relief, ca. 1915. Frame silver with scrolled design, 1.25" x 1.75". $425-575.
Bottom left: Mother-of-pearl pendant, ca. 1970. Gold metal frame, .88" x 1.25". $75-95.
Bottom center: Stone cameo pendant, ca. 1860. Frame gold metal, 1" x 1.25". $185-325.
Bottom right: Mother-of-pearl cameo pendant, ca. 1890. Silver metal frame is twisted, 1" x 1.25". $250-400.

Left: Franklin Mint glass cameo pendant with flower signed Mother's Day 1979. Sterling Silver with inlaid 24K gold frame, 1.25" x 1.62". $200-300.
Center top: Glass flower cameo brooch, ca. 1970s. Gold tone metal, 2.12" long. $65-75.
Center bottom: Shell cameo pendant with profile of woman, ca. 1930s. Gold frame with beading, .5" x .62". *Courtesy of Christie A. Stroman.* $95-125.
Right: Plastic flower clip, ca. 1970s. Gold frame, 1.5" x 2". $85-95. Unless otherwise noted, the cameos in this photograph are *Courtesy of Mary Jane Johnson.*

Top left: Florenza shell cameo earrings, ca. 1950s. Set in decorative gold frames, .75" x .75". $85-95.
Top right: Shell cameo earrings with portrait of woman, ca. 1930s. Set in twisted wire frames, .5" in diameter. $95-125.
Center left: Orange glass cameo earrings, ca. 1950s. No frames, .4" x .62". $65-75.
Center right: Glass earrings, ca. 1950s. Twisted wire frames, .5" x .62". $75-85.
Bottom left: Glass cameo clip-on earrings with green glass stones, ca. 1950s. Measures .75" x .9". $85-95.
Bottom right: Glass cameo clip-on earrings, ca. 1960s. Set in twisted wire frames, .7" x .88". $65-85.
The cameos in this photograph are *Courtesy of The Patrician Antiques.*

Opposite page:
Top left: Coro shell brooch cameo, ca. 1930s. Gold frame scalloped with flowers, 1.12" x 1.5". $175-275.
Top right: Stone cameo, ca. 1890. Gold frame 1.25" x 1.50". $325-425.
Center: Plastic Coro cameo pendant depicting mythological motif with scene of Aphrodite (Venus) and Eros (Cupid), ca. 1980s. Gold frame with twisted effect, 1.38" x 2". $45-75.
Bottom left: Stone cameo brooch of woman adorned with flowers, ca. 1900. Frame is surrounded by seed pearls entwined with twisted metal, 1.25" x 1,5". $275-295.
Bottom right: Stone cameo brooch of woman with flowers, ca. 1900. Seed pearls around gold frame, 1.25" x 1.5". $275-295.

Leather cameo pendant with portrait of man signed Italy on back, ca. 1890. Gold metal frame has twisted rope design, 1.5" x 1.62", 27" chain is more recent. $95-125.

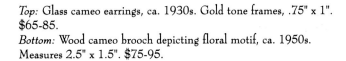

Top: Glass cameo earrings, ca. 1930s. Gold tone frames, .75" x 1". $65-85.
Bottom: Wood cameo brooch depicting floral motif, ca. 1950s. Measures 2.5" x 1.5". $75-95.

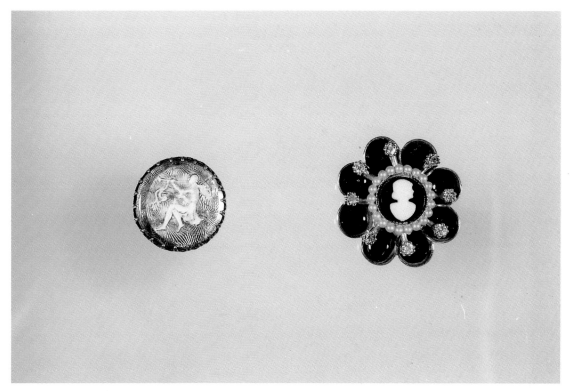

Left: Glass with painted figure on foil background, intaglio brooch depicts angel with trumpet, ca. 1900. Set on gold metal back, 1" in diameter. $125-145.

Right: White on black celluloid cameo brooch, ca. 1920-30. Black enameled frame with eight rhinestones and seed pearls on gold frame, 1.5" in diameter. $125-135.

Top: Plastic cameo brooch, ca. 1980s. Gold tone frame with pearl, .88" x 1.12". $55-65.

Center: Shell cameo brooch, ca. 1920s. Gold frame, .38" x .75". $85-120.

Bottom: Plastic cameo locket/pendant, ca. 1960s. Gold metal frame with pearls, .88" x 1.12". $85-95.

The cameos in this photograph are *Courtesy of Antiques By Daisy.*

Top: Plastic cameo pendant depicting woman with flower in hair, ca. 1930s. Gold frame, .75" x 1.25". $65-75.
Bottom: Plastic cameo pendant, ca. 1980s. Gold metal frame, 1" x 1.25". $65-75.

Watch with shell cameos of woman in profile, ca. 1960s. $65-85.
Glass ring of muse with birds, ca. 1940s. Decorative frame, 1.12" x 1.38". $45-55.
The cameos in this photograph are *Courtesy of Memory Lane Mall, Atlanta, Texas.*

Left: Plastic brooch/pendant, ca. 1980s. Gold tone frame, 1.75" x 2.12". $45-65.
Center: Black and gold glass intaglio pendant depicting floral motif, ca. 1960s. Gold metal frame, 1.88" x 2.25", and double chain, 24". $85-95.
Right: Plastic brooch/pendant with Three Muses, ca. 1980s. Gold tone frame with seed pearls, 1.62" x 1.62". $45-55.
The cameos in this photograph are *Courtesy of Cindy Porter.*

Left: Plastic brooch/pendant of woman in profile, ca. 1960s.
Elaborate frame, 1.75" x 2.25". $45-65.
Right: Glass brooch/pendant with portrait of woman, ca. 1950s.
Beaded frame, 1.62" x 2". $55-65.
The cameos in this photograph are *Courtesy of Blanche Martin.*

Top: Celluloid cameo earrings, ca. 1930s. Set in gold frames, .5" x
1". $55-85.
Bottom left and right: Plastic clip-on earrings, ca. 1950s. Etruscan
beading on frames, .75" x 1.25". $55-75.
Center bottom: Glass cameo on onyx locket, ca. 1920s. Set in gold
frame, 1.75" x 2.25". $125-175.
The cameos in this photograph are *Courtesy of Lorene Goetsch.*

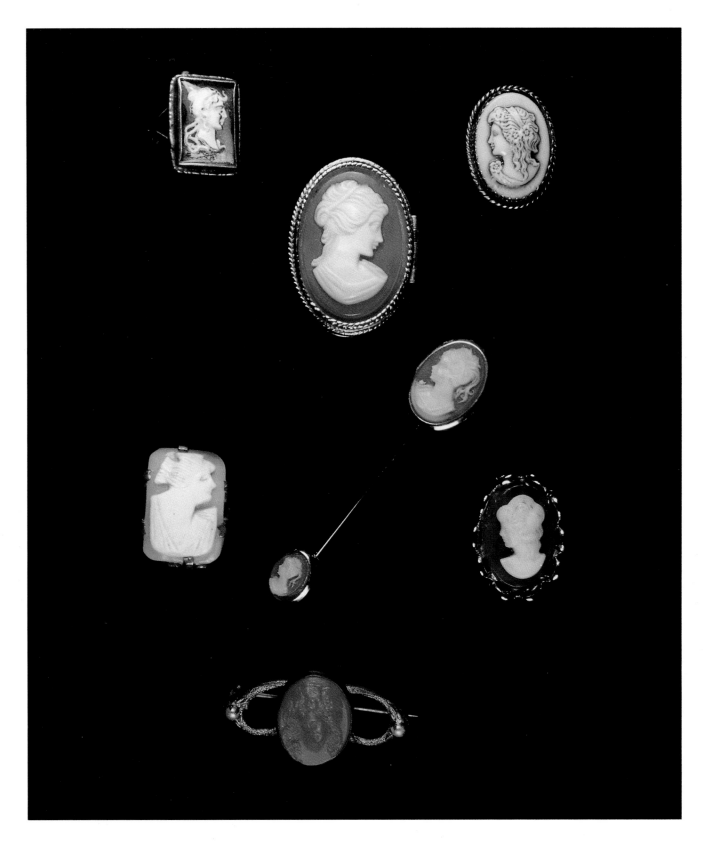

Top left: Glass over porcelain cameo ring, ca. 1880s. Sterling silver, signed England, .50" x .75" at top. $275-295.

Top center: Avon plastic cameo ring, ca. 1980s. Top opens to hold cream sachet. Gold metal, $65-85.

Top right: Ivory molded glass cameo ring, ca. 1900. Silver with twisted wire frame, .63" x .88". $275-325.

Center left: Stone cameo ring, ca. 1880. Mixed metal, .50" x .75". $350-375.

Center: Plastic stickpin with a cameo at each end, ca. 1990s. Gold metal, 2.25" long. *Courtesy of Mary Moon, Red Wagon Antiques.* $55-85.

Center right: Plastic cameo ring, ca. 1990s. Gold metal frame, .63" x .88". $35-55.

Bottom: Coral bar pin with two seed pearls, ca. 1800. Mixed metal with gold appearance, 1.25" x .75". $295-325.

Chapter Seven
Plastics

Plastic cameo of woman's portrait, ca.
1940s. Set in metal frame embossed with
flowers and leaves, measures 1.6" x 2".
$95-125.
Courtesy of Darlene Irwin.

Top: Celluloid cameo brooch, ca. 1930s.
Gold metal frame with pearls, 2.5" x 1.75".
$75-95.
Bottom: Celluloid cameo brooch, ca. 1900.
Frame and cameo molded together, 2.12" x
2.5". $125-150.
The cameos in this photograph are *Courtesy
of Sarah Newton.*

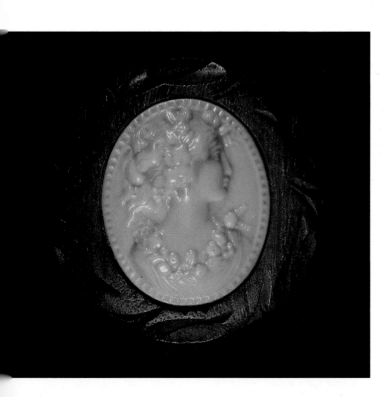

Celluloid cameo brooch depicting woman adorned with flowers, ca.
1920. Decorative wooden frame, 3" in diameter. *Courtesy of Virginia
Giles.* $95-125.

Top: Celluloid cameo brooch of woman's portrait, ca. 1890. Gold frame, 1.5" x 2.25". $95-150.
Bottom left: Celluloid cameo brooch of woman in profile with flowers in hair, ca. 1916. Gold metal frame, 1.25"-1.5". $65-100.
Bottom right: Stone cameo brooch of woman's profile, ca. 1960s. Gold frame, 1.25" x 1.68". $125-225.

Top: Celluloid cameo habillé brooch of woman's portrait with two clear stones, ca. 1916. Frame silver, 1.5" x 2". $195-250.
Center: Celluloid cameo brooch of woman with flowers in hair and on shoulder, ca. 1916. Cameo and backing molded together, 1" x 1.12". $65-85.
Bottom: Celluloid cameo brooch of woman adorned with flowers, ca. 1916. Silver frame, 1.5" x 1.88". $95-125.

Celluloid brooch, ca. 1860. Molded in one piece, 1.88" x 2.5". *Courtesy of Kathleen Cunningham*. $150-175.

Left: Celluloid cameo portrait of woman, ca. 1890s. Set in gold tone frame, measures 1.38" x 1.75". $85-95.
Center: Square celluloid cameo brooch of woman's portrait, ca. 1930. With safety clasp, measures 1.9" x 2.38". $125-150.
Right: Celluloid cameo pendant depicting woman playing mandolin, ca. 1940s. Set in beaded gold metal frame, measures 1.62" x 2". $75-95.
The cameos in this photograph are *Courtesy of The Patrician Antiques*.

Black celluloid cameo pendant of woman, ca. 1890s. Measures 2" x 2.8". *Courtesy of The Patrician Antiques*. $165-195.

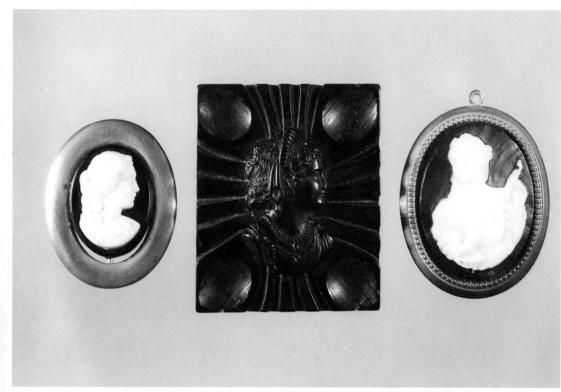

Black celluloid pendant, ca. 1890.
Measures 2.25" square. *Courtesy of Sue
Rainey Pruitt.* $95-125.

Black Bakelite cameo portrait of woman,
ca. 1920s. With celluloid chain, measures
1.88" x 2.25". *Courtesy of Frank and
Dorothy Everts.* $135-195.

Left: Jet cameo brooch, ca. 1890s. Measures 2" x 2.38". $225-250.
Right: Jet cameo brooch, ca. early 1900s. Measures 2.38" x 2.38".
$250-300.
The cameos in this photograph are *Courtesy of Antiques By Daisy*.

Left: Celluloid cameo brooch, ca. 1890. Clear background,
measures 2" x 2.38". $95-135.
Right: Celluloid cameo brooch, ca. 1890. Measures 2" x 2.38".
$125-135.

Black Bakelite cameo brooch on onyx background, ca. 1916. Gold with copper look metal frame is signed, 2.38" x 1.62". *Courtesy of Judtih M. Davis.* $125-175.

Celluloid two-toned cameo necklace with celluloid chain depicting woman, ca. 1890s. Measures 2.88" x 2.88". *Courtesy of The Patrician Antiques.* $245-295.

Top: Bakelite cameo brooch of woman in profile, ca. 1930s. Black molded, 1.75" x 2". $195-225.
Center: Obsidian cameo brooch on onyx, ca. 1915. Black enameled metal frame, 1.5" x 2". $150-175.
Bottom: Celluloid cameo pendant with white on black portrait and chain, ca. 1890. Cameo, 2.13" square, heavy chain, 26" long. $175-225.

Celluloid cameo pendant of woman's portrait, frame has scalloped edges, ca. 1890s. Measures 2.25" x 3". *Courtesy of The Patrician Antiques.* $165-225.

Top: Celluloid set on glass cameo pendant with mythological motif of Psyche depicted with butterfly wing, ca. 1900s. Set in gilt frame, measures 1.62" x 2". $200-255.
Bottom: Bakelite cameo brooch of woman in profile, ca. 1930s. Set in ornate gilt frame, measures 2" x 2.5". $195-225.
The cameos in this photograph are *Courtesy of George and Dotty Stringfield.*

White on blue celluloid cameo, ca. 1920s. Silver frame, 1" in diameter. *Courtesy of Lenora Alice Knighton.* $150-225.

Celluloid black cameo of woman's portrait, ca. 1915. Frame clear, 2.25" x 2.75". $95-125.

Top: Celluloid cameo pendant, ca. 1950s. Measures 1.4" in diameter. $85-125.
Bottom left: Celluloid cameo brooch of woman with flowers in hair and on shoulder, ca. 1930s. Measures 1.7" x 2". $85-95.
Bottom right: Celluloid cameo pendant of woman's portrait, ca. 1930s. Set in elaborate metal frame, measures 2.12" x 2.1". $95-125.
The cameos in this photograph are *Courtesy of Frank and Dorothy Everts.*

White on black celluloid plastic necklace, ca. 1880-90. Gold on rectangular frame, 1.38" x 1.75". $95-135. Courtesy of *Jerre Barkley.*

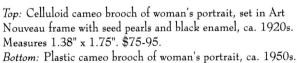

Top: Celluloid cameo brooch of woman's portrait, set in Art Nouveau frame with seed pearls and black enamel, ca. 1920s. Measures 1.38" x 1.75". $75-95.
Bottom: Plastic cameo brooch of woman's portrait, ca. 1950s. Measures 1.75" x 2.12". $55-75.
The cameos in this photograph are *Courtesy of Bobby and Mary Fyffe.*

Top left: Black on white plastic cameo brooch with bow, ca. 1930s. Set in gold metal frame, 1.25" x 1.25". $75-95.

Top right: Gold cameo pendant, ca. 1940s. Set in beaded frame, .75" x 1.5" and chain is 8.5". $65-85.

Center: Plastic cameo pendant with gold, ca. 1960s. Set in ornate gold metal frame, 2" x 2.25" and chain, 9". $65-75.

Bottom left: Glass cameo brooch, ca. 1930s. Gold tone frame, 1.5" in diameter. $85-100.

Bottom right: Glass cameo brooch, ca. 1940s. Gold frame, 1.5" x 2.88". $65-85.

The cameos in this photograph are *Courtesy of Lorene Goetsch.*

Celluloid intaglio set, ca. 1930s. Set in gold frames, earrings 1.25" x 2", brooch/pendant 1.75" x 2.25". *Courtesy of Lorene Goetsch.* $125-175.

Left: Celluloid habillé pendant with diamond, ca. 1930s. Measures 1.3" x 1.62". $75-95.
Center: Celluloid brooch, ca. 1920s. Measures .88" x 1.25". $65-75.
Right: Plastic pendant, ca. 1930s. Gold tone frame measures 1.25" x 1.75". $65-85.

Celluloid cameo brooch, ca. 1900. Celluloid frame, 1.5" x 1.88". $95-125.

Celluloid cameo clasp on pearl necklace, ca. 1930s. Cameo has gold filled frame, .62" x 1.12". *Courtesy of Antiques By Daisy.* $65-95.

Fifteen strand necklace with celluloid cameo clasp, ca. 1930s.
Cameo measures 1.25" x 1.5". *Courtesy of Shirley Falardeau.* $225-
300.

Molded milk glass cameo clip-on earrings with portrait of Psyche
with butterfly wings and hair, ca. 1930s. Gold frame with dangling
pearls, 1.12" x 1.75". *Courtesy of Jessie Surratt.* $95-125.

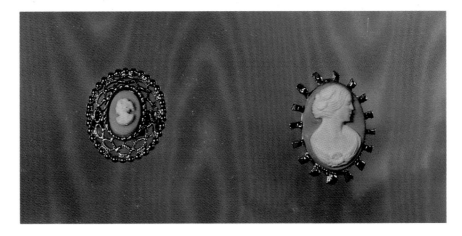

Left: Plastic Sarah Coventry brooch, ca. 1960s. Set in wire metal
frame, .88" x 1.25". $45-55.
Right: Plastic cameo brooch/pendant, ca. 1930s. Set in gold metal
frame, .88" x 1.25". $45-55.
The cameos in this photograph are *Courtesy of Lorene Goetsch.*

Left: Plastic pendant, ca. 1950. Gold metal frame and prong set cameo, 1.12" x 1.38". $45-65.
Center: Molded glass cameo pendant on agate background, ca. 1990. Gold metal frame, 1" x 1", 18" chain. $65-85.
Right: Plastic cameo locket, ca. 1950s. Gold tone frame, .62" x 1.12". $65-85.

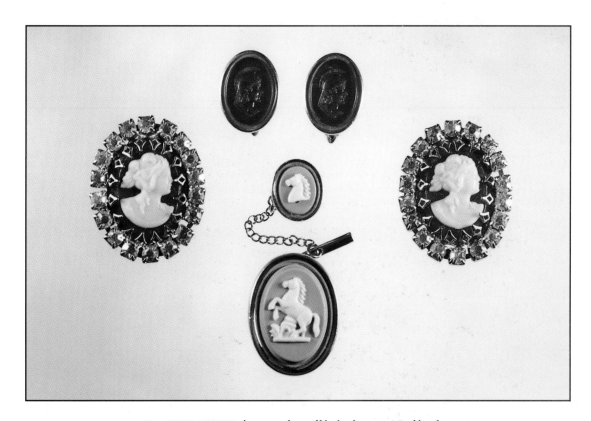

Top: KREMENTZ glass intaglio cuff links depicting profile of Classical warrior, measures .62" x .88", ca. 1950s. $75-95.
Left and right: Plastic cameo screw-on earrings with rhinestones of woman in profile, measure 1.25" x 1.5", ca. 1940s.$65-75.
Bottom: Swank cuff link of horse head, measures .5" x .62", and horse, measures .88" x 1.25", ca. 1950s. $65-75.
The cameos and intaglios in this photograph are *Courtesy of George and Dotty Stringfield.*

Top: Plastic cameo pendant of woman in profile, signed West Germany, ca. 1960s. Cameo set in frame with pearls and twisted wire, measures 1.62" x 2". $75-95.

Center: Plastic white on black cameo pendant of woman's profile, ca. 1960s. Set in beaded frame, measures .75" x 1". $55-75.

Bottom left: Circular white on black plastic cameo brooch, ca. 1950s. Set in frame of twisted and beaded wire, measures 1.25" in diameter. $85-115.

Bottom right: Loose white on black plastic cameo of woman's profile, ca. 1960s. Measures 1.2" x 1.62". $25-55.

The cameos in this photograph are *Courtesy of George and Dotty Stringfield.*

Top: Onyx earrings, signed Lewis Fegal, ca. 1960s. Set in gold frames, .5" x 1". $125-175..

Top center: Plastic cameo brooch, ca. 1920s. Gold frame with seed pearls, 1.25" in diameter. $65-85.

Bottom left and right: Onyx earrings, ca. 1940s. Frames, .5" x 1.5". $95-125.

Center bottom: Celluloid brooch cameo, ca. 1920s. Set in shell frame, 1.5" x 2.25". $125-150.

The cameos in this photograph are *Courtesy of Lorene Goetsch.*

Left: Celluloid cameo pendant depicting woman with flowers in hair, ca. 1920s. Set in beaded frame, chain made of glass beads, measures .8" x 1.12". $155-225.
Center: Plastic cameo brooch of woman's portrait, ca. 1940s. Set in Lucite frame, measures 1.38" x 2.12". $95-125.
Right top: Plastic cameo brooch depicting woman's portrait, surrounded by rhinestones, ca. 1940s. Measures 1.12" in diameter. $55-65.
Right bottom: Celluloid cameo pendant of woman's portrait, ca. 1930s. Measures .88" x 1.25". $60-70.
The cameos in this photograph are *Courtesy of The Patrician Antiques.*

Plastic cameo bracelet, ca. 1930s. Gold metal. $95-125.
Plastic cameo brooch, ca. 1930s. Silver metal frame, 1.38" in diameter. $65-75.
The cameos in this photograph are *Courtesy of Shirley Falardeau.*

Top left: Plastic cameo brooch, ca. 1940s. Set in silver frame, measures .9" x 1.25". $45-55.

Top right: Molded glass brooch, ca. 1930s. Measures 1" x 1.5". $30-40.

Center: Plastic cameo pendant and chain, ca. 1950s. Set in gold frame, measures 1.12" x 1.62". $65-85.

Bottom left: Plastic cameo habillé pendant, ca. 1930s. Measures 1.75" x 1.88". $75-95.

Bottom right: Plastic cameo brooch, ca. 1930s. Set in ornate frame, measures 1.75" x 1.62". $65-85.

The cameos in this photograph are *Courtesy of The Patrician Antiques.*

Left: Plastic cameo brooch depicting woman wearing necklace, ca. 1960s. Made in Hong Kong, measures 1.75" x 2.25". $65-75.

Center top: Plastic brooch with floral motif, ca. 1950s. Measures .88" x 1.38". $65-75.

Center Bottom: Plastic cameo brooch of woman's portrait, ca. 1950s. Set in beaded frame with twisted wire, measures 1.12" x 1.4". $75-85.

Right: Plastic cameo brooch in high relief depicting woman holding eagle, perhaps Hebe and the eagle, ca. 1950s. Braided gold frame, measures 1.75" x 2.12". $85-95.

The cameos in this photograph are *Courtesy of The Patrician Antiques.*

Top: Screwback plastic cameo earrings, ca. 1930s. Surrounded by rhinestones, .75" in diameter. $65-75.

Left bottom: Cameo plastic brooch, ca. 1950s. Set in twisted and beaded gold metal frame, 1.5" x 2". $75-85.

Center bottom: Plastic cameo, ca. 1960s. Set in scalloped gold metal frame, .75" x 1.12". $65-75.

Right bottom: Plastic cameo brooch, ca. 1950s. Set in black enamel frame with gold beading and twisted gold metal wire, 1.38" x 1.75". $75-85.

The cameos in this photograph are *Courtesy of Lorene Goetsch.*

Left: Plastic cameo brooch with beaded pearls ca. 1960s. Heavy frame measures 1.5" x 1.75". $65-75.

Center: Celluloid cameo brooch of woman, ca. 1890. Set in decorative frame, measures 1.12" x 1.38". $95-125.

Right: Plastic cameo pendant of woman, ca. 1940s. Set in twisted wire frame, measures 1.5" x 1.88". $65-75.

The cameos in this photograph are *Courtesy of The Patrician Antiques.*

Top: Plastic cameo brooch, ca. 1960s. Set in twisted gold metal wire with beading, 1.25" x 1.5". $75-95.
Center: Celluloid cameo earrings, ca. 1930s. Set in twisted gold metal wire, .75" x 2". $95-125.
Bottom: Plastic cameo pendant, ca. 1950s. Set in ornate gold metal frame, 1" x 1.5". $65-75.
The cameos in this photograph are *Courtesy of Lorene Goetsch*.

Left: Celluloid cameo brooch, ca. 1930. Measures .62" x 1.25". $65-95.
Right: Loose glass cameo, ca. 1930. Measures .88" x 1.12". $35-55.
The cameos in this photograph are *Courtesy of Louise Martin*.

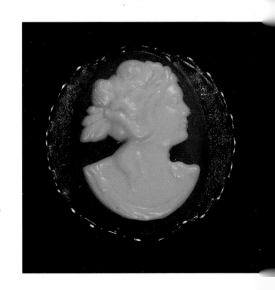

Plastic cameo brooch, ca. 1930. Applied to gold metal back, 1.25" in diameter.
Courtesy of Judith M. Davis. $45-55.

Left: Celluloid cameo pendant, ca. 1950s. Set in gold metal frame surrounded by rhinestones, 1" x 1.12". $55-65.
Center: Plastic cameo brooch of a Grecian figure, ca. 1950s. Set in decorative gold metal frame, 1.62" x 2". $95-115.
Right: Plastic cameo brooch, ca. 1960s. Set in gold metal frame, .88" x 1.12". $65-75.
The cameos in this photograph are *Courtesy of Lorene Goetsch.*

Top left and right: Celluloid earrings of woman's portrait, ca. 1940s. Set in twisted sterling silver frames, measures .5" x .62". $85-125.
Top center: Onyx cameo habillé brooch depicting woman's portrait, ca. 1920s. Set in beaded frame with glass stones and twisted wire. $250-300.
Center: Onyx cameo on celluloid background brooch, ca. 1920s. Set in decorative frame, measures .6" x .75". $150-200.
Bottom: Onyx cameo on heart shaped plastic pendant, ca. 1930s. Measures 1.2" x 1.38". $95-135.
The cameos in this photograph are *Courtesy of The Patrician Antiques.*

Black celluloid cameo brooch on white background, ca. 1890. Gold over metal frame, 1.5" x 1.75". *Courtesy of State Line Antiques Mall.* $55-65.

Top: Plastic cameo earrings, ca. 1960s. Set in gold metal frames
.62" x .75". $45-64.
Center: Cameo pendant, ca. 1960s. Set in ornate gold metal frame,
.75" x 1". $45-64.
Bottom: Plastic cameo earrings, ca. 1950s. Set in twisted gold metal
frames, .75" x .88". $65-75.
The cameos in this photograph are *Courtesy of Lorene Goetsch.*

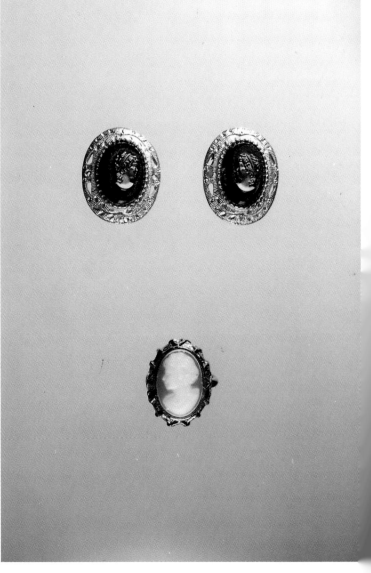

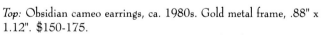

Top: Obsidian cameo earrings, ca. 1980s. Gold metal frame, .88" x
1.12". $150-175.
Bottom: Jasper ware cameo ring, ca. 1940s. Silver frame, .88" x
1.12". $95-135.
The cameos in this photograph are *Courtesy of Shirley Falardeau.*

Left: Pale pink coral cameo pendant, ca. 1930. Frame gold, 1.12" x 1.38". $225-295.
Center: White on black plastic cameo pendant, ca. 1940. Gold frame, 1.62" x 1.12". $95-125.
Right: White on black plastic cameo pendant, ca. 1950. Silver frame, .62" x 1.12". $35-45.
The cameos in this photograph are *Courtesy of Louise Martin.*

Plastic cameo bracelet clasp on pearl bracelet, ca. 1960s. Gold metal frame, 1" x 1.25". *Courtesy of Great Finds & Designs, Inc. of Texarkana.* $55-75.

Top: Plastic cameo brooch, ca. 1960s. Set in delicate twisted and beaded gold metal frame, 1.5" x 1.88". $75-85.
Bottom: STAR plastic cameo, ca. 1960s. Set in ornate, decorative gold metal frame, 2.12" x 2". $95-125.
The cameos in this photograph are *Courtesy of Lorene Goetsch.*

Left: Plastic cameo bracelet with faux diamond, ca. 1940s. Gold metal, .88" x 1.25". $65-85.
Top right: Celluloid cameo brooch, ca. 1930s. Measures .62" x .9". $45-55.
Bottom right: Plastic cameo brooch/pendant, ca. 1930s. Gold frame, 1.25" x 1.5". $55-65.
The cameos in this photograph are Courtesy of Mary Sax.

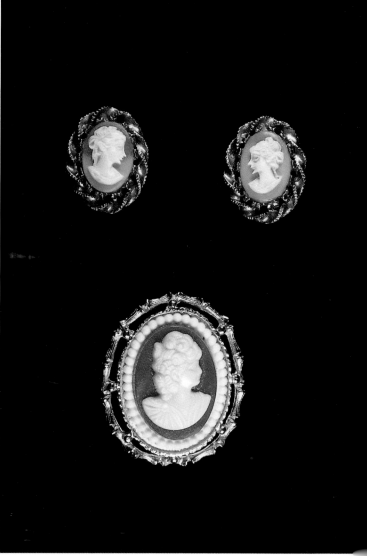

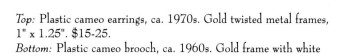

Top: Plastic cameo earrings, ca. 1970s. Gold twisted metal frames, 1" x 1.25". $15-25.
Bottom: Plastic cameo brooch, ca. 1960s. Gold frame with white beads around cameo, 1.5" x 1.75". $45-65.

Milkglass cameo brooch and earrings, ca. 1940s. Gold frame twisted on brooch, 1" x 1.25" and earrings prong set, .5" x .75". $75-150 for set.

Top: Plastic cameo pendant, ca. 1900s. Gold frame, 1.12" x 1.25". $35-75.
Bottom: Celluloid cameo pendant, ca. 1930s. Silver frame with stones around cameo, 1" in diameter. $55-75.
The cameos in this photograph are *Courtesy of Sarah Newton.*

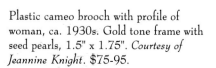

Plastic cameo brooch with profile of woman, ca. 1930s. Gold tone frame with seed pearls, 1.5" x 1.75". *Courtesy of Jeannine Knight.* $75-95.

Plastic cameo bracelet, ca. 1970s. Gold tone metal bracelet with clear stones. $65-75.

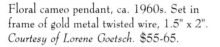

Floral cameo pendant, ca. 1960s. Set in frame of gold metal twisted wire, 1.5" x 2". *Courtesy of Lorene Goetsch.* $55-65.

Left: Plastic cameo ring, ca. 1960s. Gold tone frame, .5" x .75". $35-55.
Right: Plastic cameo brooch with flowers, ca. 1960s. Gold metal frame, 1.75" x 2.25". $55-65.
The cameos in this photograph are *Courtesy of Antiques By Daisy.*

Left: Plastic black on white cameo brooch, ca. 1960s. Set in gold metal frame, 1.5" x 1.88". $55-65.
Right: Green plastic cameo brooch with floral motif, ca. 1960s. Set in gold metal frame, 1.5" x 1.88". $55-65.
The cameos in this photograph are *Courtesy of Lorene Goetsch*.

Plastic cameo and pearl necklace, ca. 1940s. Gold frame and chain, 2" x 2.5". *Courtesy of Nell Palmer Orr*. $95-125.

Plastic Max Factor cameo locket with cream perfume depicts two women with urn on a pedestal, ca. 1960s. Gold metal frame, 1.5" x 1.88" and chain, 24.5" long. *Courtesy of Jessie Surratt*. $55-85.

Top: White on blue plastic cameo earrings of woman with flower on shoulder, ca. 1950s. Set in gold metal twisted wire frames, measure .62" x .88". $45-55.
Center: Plastic white on blue brooch/pendant of woman's portrait, ca. 1960s. Set in gold metal frame, measures 1.25" x 1.75". $45-65.
Bottom left: Shell brooch pendant depicting mythological motif of Three Muses, ca. 1940s. Set in copper beaded frame, measures 1" x 1.25". $325-450.
Bottom right: Plastic white on blue cameo brooch of woman in profile, ca. 1950s. Set in silver frame, measures .75" x 1". $65-75.
The cameos in this photograph are *Courtesy of Lorene Goetsch.*

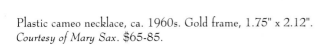

Plastic cameo necklace, ca. 1960s. Gold frame, 1.75" x 2.12".
Courtesy of Mary Sax. $65-85.

Top: Plastic brooch of woman's portrait, ca. 1950s. Set in ornate frame with tassels, brooch measures 1.5" x 2", tassels measure 2". $75-95.
Bottom: Plastic earrings of woman's portrait, ca. 1960s. Measures 1.25" x 1.5", ca. 1960s. $35-45.
The cameos in this photograph are *Courtesy of Maureen Gallagher*.

Plastic cameo brooch, ca. 1940s. Gold tone frame, 1.5" in diameter. $65-95.
Plastic cameo brooch, ca. 1940s. Gold metal frame, 1" x 1.62". $55-75.
The cameos in this photograph are *Courtesy of Lenora Alice Knighton*.

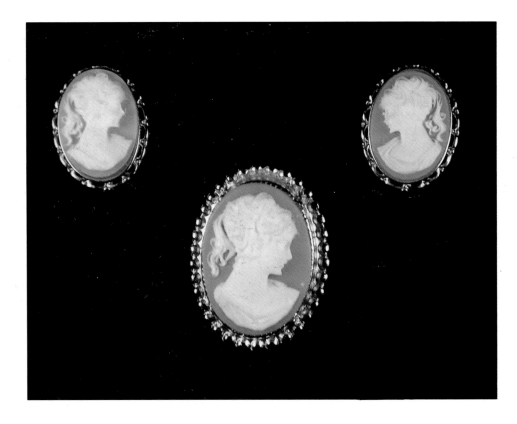

Left and right: Sarah Coventry plastic cameo earrings, ca. 1980s. Gold metal frames, .88" x .5". $55-65.
Right: Sarah Coventry plastic cameo brooch, ca. 1980s. Gold metal frame, 1" x 1.25". $75-85.
The cameos in this photograph are *Courtesy of Lenora Alice Knighton*.

Left: Plastic cameo brooch, ca. 1960s. Set in gold metal twisted and beaded wire frame, .88" x 1". $35-45.
Center: Plastic cameo locket/pendant, ca. 1950s. Set in silver metal frame, 1.75" x 2". $45-65.
Right: Cameo plastic brooch, ca. 1960s. Set in gold metal beaded frame, .75" x 1". $55-65.
The cameos in this photograph are *Courtesy of Lorene Goetsch.*

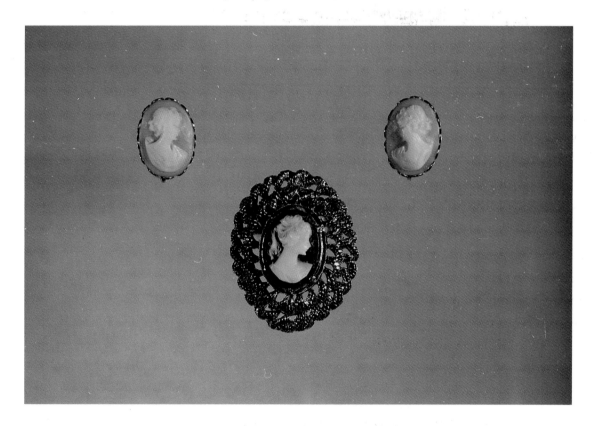

Top: Plastic cameo earrings are white with green background, ca. 1970s. Gold tone frames and backs, .62" x .88". $45-65.
Bottom: Plastic cameo brooch, ca. 1980s. Silver metal frame, 1.38" x 1.75". $55-65.
The cameos in this photograph are *Courtesy of Antiques By Daisy.*

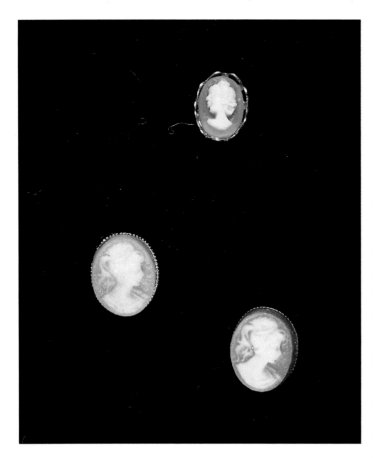

Top: Plastic cameo earring, ca. 1980s. Gold metal frame, .25" x .34". $15-25 for pair.
Bottom: Plastic cameo earrings, ca. 1980s. Gold metal frame, .34" x .5" $25-45.
The cameos in this photograph are *Courtesy of Lenora Alice Knighton*.

Top: Plastic cameo earrings, ca. 1990s. Gold metal, 1" x 1.25". $55-65.
Bottom: Plastic cameo pendant necklace, measures 1" x 1.25", ca. 1960s. $60-65.
The cameos in this photograph are *Courtesy of Mary Sax*.

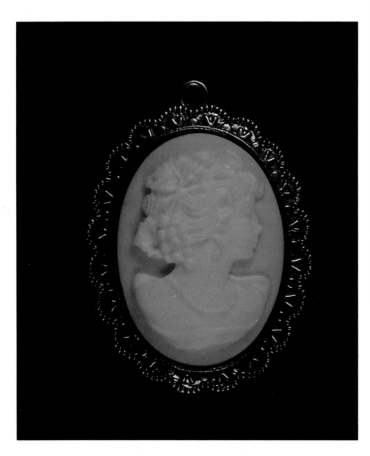

Bakelite cameo pendant depicting mythological motif of Bacchante maiden, follower of Dionysus (Bacchus) god of wine and fertility, with grapes and grape leaves in hair, ca. 1920. Gold plated frame, 1.5" x 1.75". *Courtesy of Judith M. Davis.* $95-125.

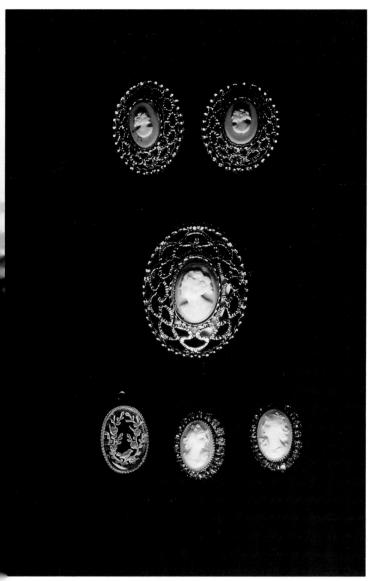

Top: Plastic cameo earrings and brooch/pendant set signed Sarah Coventry, ca. 1980s. White on blue with gold metal frames, earrings .88" x 1.12", and brooch/pendant 1.25" x 1.5". $125-150.
Bottom left: Glass intaglio pendant, ca. 1990s. Wreath design etched from reverse with gold metal frame, .62" x .75". $20-35.
Bottom right: Stone cameo earrings with marcasites around, ca. 1920s, .62" x .75". Sterling silver $295-325.

Top: Plastic floral earrings, ca. 1960s. Set in gold metal frame, .62" x .88". $15-25.
Center: Plastic cameo brooch of the Three Muses, Western Germany, ca. 1960s. Set in decorative silver metal frame, 1.62" x 2". $65-75.
Bottom: Cameo earrings, ca. 1970s. Set in elegant silver metal frames, 1.25" x 1.5". $75-85.
The cameos in this photograph are *Courtesy of Lorene Goetsch*.

Left: Plastic cameo brooch, ca. Molded as one piece, 1.75" in diameter. $25-45.
Right: Glass cameo brooch, ca. 1960s. Gold frame, 1.38" x 1.5". $55-95.
The cameos in this photograph are *Courtesy of Shirley Falardeau*.

Top: Celluloid cameo earrings, ca. 1930s, .65" x 75". Set in beaded frames with rhinestones, $45-65.
Bottom: Plastic earrings and necklace depicting mythological motif of Bacchante maiden, follower of Dionysus (Bacchus), god of wine and fertility, ca. 1960s. Each cameo measures 1" x 1.25". $65-75.
The cameos in this photograph are *Courtesy of Elizabeth Smith*.

Top: Avon plastic pendant/locket was Top Avon Honor Award which held Rapture Perfume, ca. 1966 Presidents Campaign. Gold tone metal, 1.38" x 1.75". $75-95.

Center left: Plastic cameo brooch depicting mythological motif of Aphrodite (Venus) and Eros (Cupid), ca. 1970s. Silver metal with twisted wire around edge, 1.38" x 1.75". $65-75.

Center right: Plastic cameo brooch of man and woman, ca. 1970s. Silver metal frame, 1.25" x 1.62". $65-75.

Bottom: Plastic cameo brooch with Three Muses, ca. 1960s. Frame is metal with white enameling, 1.5" x 1.88. $75-95.

Top: Plastic cameo earrings, ca. 1950s. Set in gold metal frames, .75" x 1". $65-85.

Bottom: Plastic cameo pendant, ca. 1950s. Set in ornate gold metal frame with pearls, 1.25" x 2", chain 12". $85-95.

The cameos in this photograph are *Courtesy of Lorene Goetsch.*

Left: Plastic cameo brooch of woman's portrait with dark background, ca. 1960s. Measures 1.25" x 1.62". $35-45.
Center: Shell cameo pendant of woman, ca. 1940s. Set in twisted wire frame with chain and linked metal frame, measures .6" x .75". $295-350.
Right: Plastic cameo pendant of woman, ca. 1960s. Set in twisted wire frame, measures 1.12" x 1.5". $75-85.
The cameos in this photograph are *Courtesy of Lenora Alice Knighton*.

Left and right: Plastic cameo clip-on earrings depicting mythological motif of Three Muses, ca. 1960s. Set in angular gold metal frames, 1" x 1.12". $45-64.
Center: Plastic cameo brooch depicting mythological motif of Aphrodite (Venus) and Eros (Cupid), ca. 1960s. Set in twisted and beaded gold metal frame, 1.5" x 1.88". $65-75.
The cameos in this photograph are *Courtesy of Lorene Goetsch*.

Left: Whiting Davis plastic pendant with floral motif, ca. 1970s. Set in silver metal frame, 1.75" x 2.25". $75-85.
Right: Plastic floral brooch/pendant, ca. 1970s. Set in silver metal frame, 2" x 2.25". $65-75.
The cameos in this photograph are *Courtesy of Lorene Goetsch.*

Plastic cameo with white flowers on blue background signed GERRY, ca. 1970s. Gold plated frame, 1.5" x 2". *Courtesy of Garden Gate Antiques.* $65-75.

Plastic cameo locket/music box/pendant of woman with flower on shoulder, marked Sankyo, ca. 1960s. Gold frame measures 1.75" x 1.88". *Courtesy of Bobby and Mary Fyffe.* $85-95.

Plastic cameo of woman in profile, ca. 1960s. Set in decorated frame, measures 1.25" x 1.62". *Courtesy of Maureen Gallagher.* $85-95.

Top: Shell cameo clip-on earrings, ca. 1950s. Set in gold metal frames, .75" x 1". $125-150.
Bottom: Plastic cameo necklace, ca. 1950s. Set in gold frame with pearls, .88" x 1.62", chain 14". $65-85.
The cameos in this photograph are *Courtesy of Lorene Goetsch.*

Left: Plastic cameo brooch, ca. 1960s. Set in gold metal frame, 1.25" x 1.5". $75-85.
Center: Plastic cameo pendant, ca. 1960s. Set in twisted, ornate gold metal frame, 1.38" x 1.5". $75-95.
Right: Plastic cameo brooch, ca. 1960s. Set in twisted gold metal frame, 1.12" x 1.38". $65-75.
The cameos in this photograph are *Courtesy of Lorene Goetsch.*

Top: Brown plastic cameo, ca. 1960s. Set in ornate gold metal frame, 1.62" x 1.12". $15-25.
Bottom left: Blue plastic cameo, ca. 1960s. Set in ornate gold metal frame, 1.62" x 1.12". $15-25.
Bottom right: Green plastic cameo, ca. 1960s. Set in ornate gold metal frame, 1.62" x 1.12". $15-25.
The cameos in this photograph are *Courtesy of Lorene Goetsch.*

Top: Tiny cameo plastic earrings, ca. 1960s. Set in gold metal frames, .44" x .5". $35-45.
Center left: Plastic cameo pendant, ca. 1960s. Set in heavy gold metal frame, .75" x 1". $45-64.
Center right: Plastic cameo pendant, ca. 1940s. Set in scalloped gold metal frame, .44" x .88". $65-75.
Bottom left: Plastic cameo pendant, ca. 1930s. Set in twisted gold metal frame, .88" x 1.25". $55-75.
Bottom center: Plastic heart cameo pendant/locket, ca. 1960s. Set in gold metal frame, .62" x .75". $65-75.
Bottom right: Plastic cameo pendant, ca. 1960s. Set in unusual gold metal frame, 1" x 1.5". $75-85.
The cameos in this photograph are *Courtesy of Lorene Goetsch.*

Top: Plastic cameo earrings, ca. 1960s. Set in gold frames, .5" x .75". $45-55.
Bottom: Coro plastic cameo necklace, ca. 1960s. Set in elegant gold metal frame, 1.25" x 1.5", gold metal chain 10.5". $85-95.
The cameos in this photograph are *Courtesy of Lorene Goetsch.*

Left: Plastic cameo earrings, ca. 1960s. Set in decorative gold metal frames, .75" x .88". $55-75.
Center: Plastic cameo brooch/pendant, ca. 1960s. Set in twisted, circular gold metal frame, 1.38" x 1.75". $75-85.
Right: Plastic cameo earrings, ca. 1960s. Set in gold metal frames, .62" x .75". $55-75.
The cameos in this photograph are Courtesy of Lorene Goetsch.

Top: Plastic cameo brooch, ca. 1980s. Gold metal frame, 1.5" x 2". $45-65.
Bottom: Plastic cameo earrings, ca. 1980s. Gold metal frame, .88" x 1.25". $35-45.

Left: Coro plastic molded cameo pendant, ca. 1960s. Gold frame, 1.75" x 2" and chain, 48". $85-95.
Center: Plastic cameo brooch/pendant, ca. 1960s. Gold frame, 2" x 2.25". $65-75.
Right: Plastic cameo pendant, ca. 1960s. Gold frame, 1.25" x 1.75". $45-55.

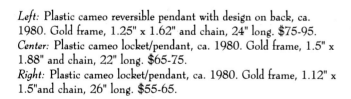

Left: Plastic cameo reversible pendant with design on back, ca. 1980. Gold frame, 1.25" x 1.62" and chain, 24" long. $75-95.
Center: Plastic cameo locket/pendant, ca. 1980. Gold frame, 1.5" x 1.88" and chain, 22" long. $65-75.
Right: Plastic cameo locket/pendant, ca. 1980. Gold frame, 1.12" x 1.5"and chain, 26" long. $55-65.

Left: Plastic brooch with two women and vase on pedestal, ca. 1970.
Frame gold tone, 1.5" x 1.88". $45-75.
Center: Plastic pendant, ca. 1970. Gold metal frame with white
enameling and pearls, 1.38" x 1.75", 24" chain. $45-75.
Right: Plastic brooch, ca. 1980. Gold metal frame, 1.5" x 2". $45-
65.

Four pair of plastic cameo earrings, ca. 1950-80. All have gold
metal frames and backs. $25-65.

Assortment of plastic cameo earrings, ca. 1960-90. Life size photograph. *Courtesy of Great Finds & Designs, Inc. of Texarkana.* $20-65.

Assortment of plastic cameo earrings, ca. 1960-80. Life size photograph. *Courtesy of Great Finds & Designs, Inc. of Texarkana.* $25-65.

Two necklaces with plastic cameos, ca. 1990s. Gold metal pendants, 2.38" x 2.5". *Courtesy of Great Finds & Designs, Inc. of Texarkana.* $45-65.

Plastic cameo brooch, ca. 1980. Gold frame with pearls, 1.75" in diameter. $45-75.

Left: Plastic cameo brooch, ca. 1980s. Gold metal frame, 1.75" x 2". $65-75.
Right: Unframed Bakelite cameo, ca. 1920. Measures 1.5" x 2". $125-150.
The cameos in this photograph are *Courtesy of Cindy Porter.*

Speidel plastic cameo bracelet and necklace in box, ca. 1960s.
Courtesy of Sarah Newton. $125-155.

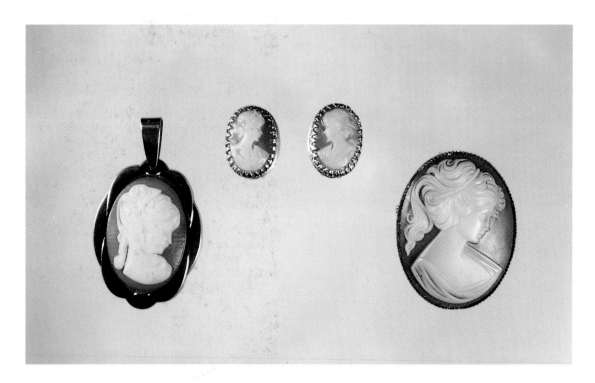

Left: Plastic cameo pendant of woman's portrait, ca. 1960s. Set in
gold frame, measures 1.12 x 1.5". $65-85.
Center: Whiting Davis plastic cameo clip-on earrings, depicting
women with flowers in their hair, ca. 1960s. Measure .62" x .75".
$45-65.
Right: Plastic cameo brooch depicting woman with flowing hairstyle,
ca. 1960s. Measures 1.25" x 1.62". $25-35.
The cameos in this photograph are *Courtesy of George and Dotty
Stringfield.*

Plastic cameo pendant/locket depicting woman's portrait, measures 1.75" x 2", ca. 1960s. *Courtesy of Patsy W. Poulos.* $65-75.

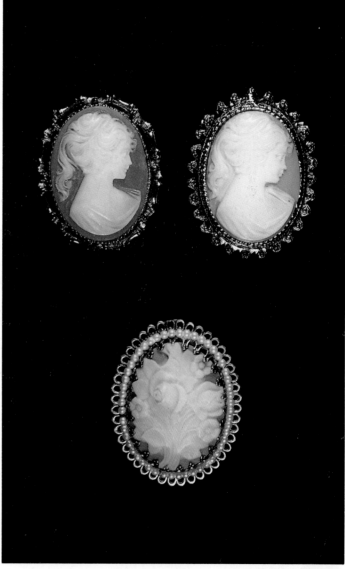

Top left: Unsigned white on coral plastic cameo brooch, ca. 1960s. Gold tone frame, 1.25" x 2". $55-65.
Top right: Unsigned white on blue plastic cameo brooch, ca. 1960s. Gold tone frame with beading, 1.25" x 2". $55-65.
Bottom: Unsigned white on green plastic cameo brooch with flower, ca. 1960s. Gold and pearl frame, 1.25" x 2". $55-65.
The cameos of this photograph are *Courtesy of Lenora Alice Knighton.*

Left: White on green plastic cameo locket, c. 1980s. Set in gold tone frame, 2" in diameter. $45-65.
Right: Glass on onyx cameo locket, ca. 1960s. Set in gold metal frame, 1.75" x 2". $125-150.
The cameos in this photograph are *Courtesy of Lorene Goetsch.*

Left: Plastic white on black brooch with anonymous woman, ca. 1950s. Measures 1.25" x 1.62". $45-55.
Right: White on orange plastic brooch of woman, signed Hong Kong, ca. 1960s. Gold frame, 1.12" x 1.38". $55-65.
The cameos in this photograph are *Courtesy of Sandy Burnett.*

Left: Blue and white plastic cameo bracelets, ca. 1990s. Gold metal. $35-55.
Right: Plastic pendant cameo. Silver frame, 1.25" x 1.75". $65-75.
The cameo bracelets in this photograph are *Courtesy of Great Finds & Designs, Inc. of Texarkana.*

Cameo necklace with locket and chains, plastic cameo ca. 1960s. Set in twisted wire frame and measures .88" x 1". *Courtesy of The Patrician Antiques*. $75-95.

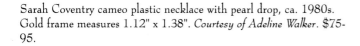

Sarah Coventry cameo plastic necklace with pearl drop, ca. 1980s. Gold frame measures 1.12" x 1.38". *Courtesy of Adeline Walker*. $75-95.

Left: Plastic cameo brooch, ca. 1960s. Set in twisted silver metal frame, 1.5" x.1.88". $45-55.
Center: Heart shaped plastic cameo pendant, ca. 1960s. Set in silver metal frame, .75" x .75". $25-35.
Right: Plastic cameo brooch, PERI, ca. 1960s. Set in decorative silver metal frame, 1.38" x 1.62". $55-65.
The cameos in this photograph are *Courtesy of Lorene Goetsch.*

Plastic cameo pendant, ca. 1960s. Set in large, ornate gold frame, 2.5" x 4". *Courtesy of Lorene Goetsch.* $75-95.

Left: Plastic brooch of two muses, ca. 1940s. Set in braided frame, 1.5" x 1.88". $35-45.
Right: Plastic compact/pillbox with man and woman, ca. 1940s. 2" in diameter. $55-65.
The brooch and compact/pillbox in this photograph are *Courtesy of Sandy Burnett.*

Top: Plastic cameo compact , ca. 1940s. White on dark blue with gold metal, 2" in diameter. $75-95.
Bottom left: Plastic cameo pendant/locket, ca. 1990s. White on blue with gold metal frame, 1.5" x 1.88". $75-95.
Bottom right: Plastic brooch, ca. 1970s. White on blue with gold frame, 1.88" x 2". $45-65.

Plastic brooch with scene of man and woman, ca. 1960. No frame, 1.25" x 1.88". *Courtesy of Louise Martin.* $45-65.

Left: Plastic cameo brooch, ca. 1980s. Gold frame, 1.5" x 1.38". $55-65.
Center: Plastic cameo pendant with two faces, ca. 1990s. Gold metal frame, 2.25" x 2.75". $75-95.
Right: Plastic cameo brooch, ca. 1980s. Gold frame, 1.25" x 1.75". $55-65.
The cameos in this photograph are *Courtesy of Great Finds & Designs, Inc. of Texarkana.*

Left: Plastic white on coral background brooch, ca. 1980s. Gold frame, 1.88" x 2.5". $45-65.
Right: Plastic brooch, ca. 1980s. Twisted gold metal frame, 1.5" x 2". $45-65.

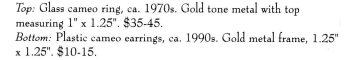

Top: Glass cameo ring, ca. 1970s. Gold tone metal with top measuring 1" x 1.25". $35-45.
Bottom: Plastic cameo earrings, ca. 1990s. Gold metal frame, 1.25" x 1.25". $10-15.

White on black plastic cameo brooch depicting two muses, ca. 1960s. Gold metal frame, 1.44" x 1.88". *Courtesy of Jessie Surratt.* $65-75.

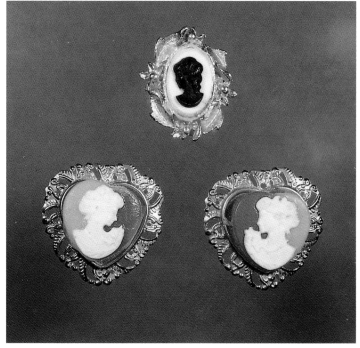

Top: Plastic cameo necklace, ca. 1950s. Backing clear Lucite butterfly with green stones in shape of flower, 2.12" x 2.12". $45-65.

Center left: Plastic cameo pendant necklace with portrait of woman with flower on shoulder, ca. 1970s. Reversible with gold-tone pendant with design on reverse, 1.25" x 1.5", chain 24" long. $65-85.

Center right: Avon plastic cameo brooch depicting floral motif, ca. 1980s. Frame and cameo molded together, 1.25" x 1.5. $65-75.

Bottom left: Plastic cameo earrings, ca. 1980s. No frame, .75" x 1". $45-55.

Bottom center: Plastic cameo earrings, ca. 1930s. Gold frames, .38" x .88". $55-65.

Bottom right: .Plastic cameo necklace signed 1920, ca. 1950s. Gold frame, .75" x 1.25"and chain, 20". $55-75.

Top left: Avon plastic stick pin, ca. 1970s. Gold tone. $45-75.
Top right: Sarah Coventry cameo ring, ca. 1950s. $35-55.
Bottom left: Sarah Coventry cameo pendant and chain, ca. 1960s. $55-75.
Bottom right: Cameo pendant with pearl drop, ca. 1970s. $65-85.
The cameos in this photograph are *Courtesy of Virginia Young.*

Glossary

Agate A form of chalcedony with bands of color or irregular clouding.

Amber A substance of brown, yellow, red, orange, gray, or green fossil resin that is translucent and commonly found along the Baltic Shores.

Amethyst A type of quartz that is transparent; it is purple or violet in color.

Art Deco Refers to the period from 1910 through 1930 when there was an interest centered around modern art movements. Angular lines in jewelry were popular at this time.

Art Nouveau A period between 1890 to 1910 during which fluid lines were prominent in jewelry. Some popular motifs were dragonflies, mourning glories, and women depicted with long, flowing hair.

Bakelite The trademark name of a group of thermosetting plastics that have a high resistance to heat. Formulated by Belgian chemist, L. H. Bakeland, in 1909.

Bezel A groove or flange that encircles a gem to hold it in its setting.

Book Chain A necklace made of square or rectangular links which was popular from the 1850s to the 1890s.

Bracelet A piece of jewelry that encircles the wrist.

Brooch A decorative pin.

Cameo A portrait or scene that is carved in relief. Cameos have been molded from natural materials and synthetics.

Cameo Habillé A cameo portrait adorned with jewelry such as a necklace and/or earrings and diadem that contained one or more diamonds.

Carnelian A type of clear chalcedony that varies from pale to deep red or reddish brown.

Cast A mold of an original piece done in plaster of paris.

Celluloid Trademarked in 1869 by John Wesley Hyatt, this flammable material is colorless and made of nitrocellulose and camphor.

Chalcedony A transparent quartz found in various colors, often in milky or gray.

Coral Made by marine organisms called polyps which attach themselves to an object and eventually die, leaving thier skeletons behind. Over a period of years, the polyps form coral. Color ranges from pink to red as well as black and white.

Costume jewelry Refers to popular jewelry made of non-precious materials.

Crystal A mineral that is clear and transparent and resembles ice.

Cut Steel Beads resembling marcasites.

Demi-Parure Consists of two or three matching pieces in a set.

Depose French word meaning "patent" or "copyright."

Diadem A decorated headband which resembles a tiara.

Diamond Extremely hard and valuable gem made of pure carbon, usually clear, but can be found in yellow, blue, black, or green.

Die Stamping A process used in mass production of jewelry in which a design is cut in metal.

Engraving A method of cutting lines into metal.

Etruscan Refers to jewelry a style of jewelry originated by the ancient Etruscans in Italy from the 6th and 7th centuries. The jewelry saw a revival in the 19th century. Patterns of small gold beads on a gold background characterize Etruscan jewelry. Fornutato Pio Castellani, an Italian 19th century jeweler, is given credit for reviving the Etruscan style of jewelry.

Faux In French, this word means "false."

Filigree A procedure in which fine wire has been twisted into a lace or web like pattern.

Fob Attached to a watch chain, this ornament was popular from the 1890s through the 1930s. Fobs experienced a revival with the renewed popularity of the pocket. Some fobs were set with intaglios or cameos.

French Jet Refers to jewelry made of black glass.

Georgian Refers to the period from 1714 to 1830 during which England was ruled by four of the Georges.

Gold-Filled Comprised of a base metal with an outer layer of gold.

Granulation Decoration of a metal surface using tiny grains or gold beads. This process is a characteristic of Etruscan jewelry, revived in the nineteenth century.

Gutta-percha Made from the latex of tropical trees and used frequently during the nineteenth century.

Hallmark A mark incised, stamped, or punched on silver or gold to show sterling or "carat" according to standards set by country of origin. Some require other information such as manufacturer, patent, and origin.

Hematite An iron ore which can be red or brown. The crystals are found mostly in men's jewelry.

High Relief Used to describe a cameo in which the carving rises up from the background and creates a three dimensional look.

Intaglio A process opposite of cameo in which the artist carves into the stone below the surface.

Ivory The yellowish, white, smooth substance that is hard and comes from the tusks of elephants. Often used to describe tusks from other animals or bone.

Jet Used commonly in the nineteenth century, this substance was mined in Whitby, England, and was a type of fossilized coal.

Karat (Carat) The weight of gems and gemstones or gold as set by a standard scale.

Lapis A gemstone of deep blue that sometimes has small iron pyrite flecks.

Lava A common substance for cameos in the early to late 1800s, lava from Pompeii ranged from a cream color, dark greens, dark brown, black, and white. The softness of the material allowed carvers to create beautiful high relief carvings.

Locket A piece of jewelry that functions as a pendant and/or a brooch and contains a compartment for a photograph or hair and a cover.

Lyre Most closely associated with Apollo, this musical instrument resembles a harp.

Marcasite A hard, white iron pyrite that is cut and set into sterling silver.

Moonstone A feldspar known for its pearly translucent color.

Mother-of-Pearl The internal layer of mollusk shells that is iridescent in color.

Mounting A backing or a setting for a cameo or other piece of jewelry.

Opal A translucent and sometimes iridescent gem composed of hydrated silicon dioxide.

Parure A set which commonly includes a matching necklace, earrings, brooch, and bracelet.

Pate-de-Verre Heavy paste glass in muted colors; produced from crystal and lead ground into paste, molded, and fired in a kiln.

Pendant A suspended piece of jewelry attached to a necklace or bracelet.

Pinchbeck A substance is made from an alloy of zinc to imitate gold. Created by Christopher Pinchbeck (1670-1732), a London alchemist, jeweler, and watchmaker.

Plastic Synthetic products made from chemicals which could be molded or carved into shapes and fashioned into jewelry. Early plastics proved impractical because of flammability, but celluloid was used during the Victorian era, and Bakelite followed in the early 1900s.

Relief The projection of a figure from a flat background.

Repoussé A method of decorating metal where a design is pushed out from the back to stand out in relief on the front.

Rhinestone A clear, imitation stone that has the sparkle of a diamond and is made of paste or glass.

Seed Pearl A small pearl often used on frames of cameos.

Setting A mounting for a cameo or other piece of jewelry.

Stick Pin Pin popular with men from around 1870 to the early 1900s. The pin was worn on a tie and had a small decorative piece at the top.

Topaz An aluminum silicate mineral prized as a gemstone that varies in color from light yellow to deep orange.

Tortoiseshell The covering of a sea turtle which is brown and translucent; used to make combs and jewelry.

Vermeil Bronze copper or silver gilded and varnished to give a piece high luster. Usually a gold wash over silver.

Victorian Era The years of Queen Victoria's reign (1837-1901). Queen Victoria's love of jewelry made it popular during her reign.

Wedgwood English firm began by Josiah Wedgwood. Through the production of jaspar ware in blues and whites or greens and whites, the firm made hundreds of cameos as well as cuff links, rings, tie pins, and pendants. The motifs most often used were mythological.

Bibliography

Baker, Lillian. *100 Years of Collectible Jewelry*. Paducah, Kentucky: Collector Books, 1993.

Bell, Jeanenne. *Answers to Questions About Old Jewelry 1840-1950*. Florence, Alabama: Books Americana Inc., 1985.

Darling, Ada. *Antique Jewellry*. Watkins Glen, New York: Century House, 1953.

Flower, Margaret. *Victorian Jewellry*. South Brunswick and New York: A.S. Barnes and Company, 1973.

Gere, Charlotte. *Victorian Jewellry Design*. Chicago: Henry Regnery Company, 1972.

Henig, Martin. *Classical Gems: Ancient and Modern Intaglios in Fitzwilliam Museum Cambridge*. Cambridge: Cambridge University Press, 1994.

Kaplan, Guy. *The Official Identification and Price Guide to Antique Jewelry*. New York: Random House, 1990.

Kelley, Lyngerda, and Nancy Schiffer. *Plastic Jewelry*. West Chester, Pennsylvania: Schiffer Publishing, Ltd., 1987.

Mastai, Marie-Louise d'Otrange. *Jewelry*. The Smithsonian Institution's National Museum of Design: Cooper-Hewitt Museum, 1981.

Miller, Anna M. *The Buyer's Guide to Affordable Antique Jewelry*. New York: Citadel Publishing Group, 1995.

Miller, Anna M. *Cameos Old and New*. New York: Van Nostrand Reinhold, 1991.

Sunderland, Beth Benton. *The Romance of Seals and Engraved Gems*. New York: The Macmillan Company, 1965.

Index

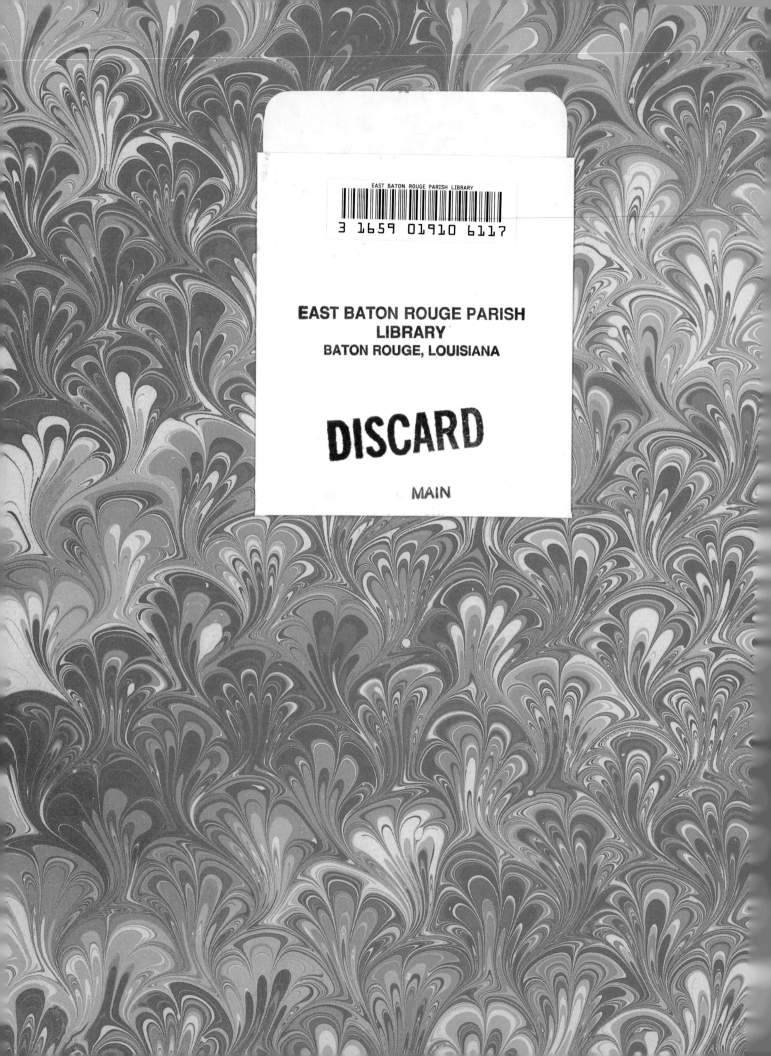